Look Through the Window

A. Ware

The main story in this book is based on true events.

Names have been changed to protect the innocent and/or those involved. Where a few real names are used, and some of them are deceased, their names are mentioned in this book in their honor.

(Deborah Lundy, Robert E. Portis, Leavator Ryans, Gloria Casey, Sylvia Wilson, Mary Coleman, and Gertie Perkins)

Published by: Arnita L. Ware

www.justwrite4insight.com

ISBN-13: 979-8-9944384-0-4 (Hardcover)
ISBN-13: 979-8-9944384-1-1 (Paperback)
ISBN-13: 979-8-9944384-2-8 (ebook)

This book is dedicated to my loving Mother, (the one and only) Arbiezean Ryans Portis, who encouraged me to pray about everything, to be an individual, to be a trendsetter.
Her famous words…
"You don't follow the crowd, you let the crowd follow you!"

~Arbiezean Portis

I Love You, Mama.

Vernis Ware,
Thank you for putting up with me during the season of working on this book (1st Edition) … leaving me alone, and allowing me time to write!

Others who have absolutely encouraged me on this writing journey who are dear friends and/or family…Thank you so much!

My Cousin Larry D. Johnson & His daughter, Chantell (Ms. Beauty)
Cousin Ethel M. LaBostrie & Aunt Louise Portis

Gone but not forgotten…

Ms. Leavator Ryans (Aunt Lee)
Mrs. Evelyn B. Spears (Grandma Spears)

To my lifelong childhood friend, Mr. Tommy Charles Badon, Sr.
My best friend since middle school, First Lady…Mrs. Denise M. Wilson
Ms. Sharon D. Oliver & Ms. Cynthia A. Yates
Mr. King

The World's Greatest High School English Teacher… Ms. Katie Rovaris
Institute for Writer's Instructor… Mrs. Lynn Smith
Cafe' Confidential….Writing Coach . . . Mr. Steve Roller

Other Acknowledgements . . .

Table of Contents

Acknowledgments

If it had not been for the Lord who was on my side, I don't know where I would be.

Thank you, Lord for choosing me to chronicle my life story for such a time as this.

To my wonderful, loving, and supportive family... I could not have done this without you.

Mother & Sisters (Linda & Roben)

My Three Sons (Leon, Jeremy & Larry & Daughters-in-love.)

To all of my other dear friends, I appreciate you, too.

To my spiritual leaders,
Bishop R. L. Sample & The Late First Lady Dollie V. Sample
&
Eld. Perry Williams & First Lady Norma Williams
my church family…(Holy Tabermacle Church, Fort Worth, TX)

"Thanks a million X infinity" . . . for keeping me lifted in prayer.

Last, but not least much love to ALL of Mimi's babies who bring me SO much joy!

I Love You Forever,
Arnita

Lisa Bell (Editor) - Radical Women

We did it! 😊 Thank you & much love!

Karen Austin (Book Cover Designer)

Your artistic taste is meticulous. It appears we believe in **aesthetics** *& the* ***"philosophy of beauty"****…studying and choosing all things beautiful, just like our* **Creator**.

The collaboration was smooth. Talk about satisfaction guaranteed.

You did that!

Anita's Story

Introduction

When I was a young girl, we used to play a game called 'Connect the dots'.

Experience taught me that everything happens for a reason.

All of my experiences have been connected. "*To everything there is a season, a time and a purpose under the heaven.*" (Ecclesiastes 3:1, KJV) I had to learn to accept that in some areas of my life, the season is up!

I choose to tell my story hoping to help at least one soul. I choose to be transparent, even at the risk of exposing the truths of my own life. All of us have skeletons, or have had skeletons, of some kind in the closet—maybe areas we might not ordinarily share with the world. Well, I've known for many, many years I was chosen to share my story with the world. Where it will lead me, I do not know, but I pray my story comes to life and speaks to areas in yours—even at the risk of you going down memory lane to clear and cleanse your heart of unsolved issues.

Yes, you may have stuck your head in the sand and pretended those issues no longer exist, but in reality, you've not dealt with them. This book is especially dedicated to you!

I know some of you can relate to my experiences. I pray you can accept my courage to share my life with you. I refuse to let my past hurts, pains, wrongs and injustices define me.

I choose to look ahead and stay focused on the goals and dreams God planted in me. Let me be perfectly clear, I will be the first to disclose that I have not been a true "saint" during all of my days as a believer. Nor do I make *any* excuses for wrongs I may have committed or permitted against anyone. All I can say is that we should learn and grow from our experiences.

Since, I have only one *judge*, I'm not concerned about how people may feel about me or what they may think after reading this book. All I know is I am on a divine assignment concerning my own life. You may choose to live your life as you see fit. We will all have to answer and give an account of our lives. As for me, when I leave this earth, I want my heart and conscience to be clear that I have reconciled myself with others, as well as my Creator.

May I suggest you do the same? I also suggest you make peace with people where you need to. If you owe someone an apology, you should apologize. If you need to forgive someone, you should forgive. And if you need to ask for forgiveness, please do so. Finally, if you need to say, "I love you," do it quickly!

Weeping may endure for a night, but joy comes in the morning. I choose "joy!" My morning has come!

From my heart to yours,

A. Ware

Chapter 1 – The Early Years

Lost, But Now I'm Found

Do you believe in angels? I believe! I'm living proof that angels watched over me.

When I was only about 3 years old, I got lost. How does a 3-year-old manage to get lost?

> *"Nothing is impossible with God."*
>
> *Luke 1:37*

As the story goes, I'm told, that I was being watched by my sibling and cousins. They decided to sneak off to the corner store while I napped. Honestly though, the process for someone so young, I should say—I slept, and surely they'd be back way before I woke up. I know they were just kids being kids. I blame no one. Besides, it was all a part of a bigger plan.

Apparently, before they returned, I woke up and managed to walk out of the apartment and cross several streets. Somewhere way in the back of my memory, I remember looking up at a really tall building. I stood in front of a high-rise building, which was a nursing-home facility.

Thankfully, for everyone's sake, I was safely returned to our house by a friend of one of my cousins, who recognized me. It could have been so much worse. I don't know about you, but when I reflect over that specific circumstance, it makes me realize God's hand was upon my life, even at an early age.

My First Experience of Death

Who remembers how old they were when they had their first experience of death with a close family member? I do!

> *"Character cannot be developed in ease and quiet. Only through experiences of trial and suffering can the soul be strengthened, vision cleared, ambition inspired, and success achieved."*
>
> *Helen Keller*

When I was six years old, I lost a very dear family member, due to a drowning. Her name was Deborah, we called her Debbie. I was quite close to her. She was my first cousin, and I was always around her as a little girl.

We used to spend the night at my aunt's house on a regular basis. We'll call her Aunt Lavonne. The last time I saw Debbie alive, she was rushing off that day back to Mississippi, since she recently moved there.

Her sister, who I will call Evelyn said to her, "Wait Debbie, don't go. Please don't go. Just stay for the rest of the week.."

Evelyn had just graduated high school on Tuesday, and wanted Debbie to stay through the weekend. And, she had a bad feeling about her leaving, having had a vision about her drowning.

Evelyn and I were standing in the hallway of the apartments looking out the window, as she drove away saying, "I can't wait Evelyn, I've gotta go, I've got to go!"

It was as if she was in a hurry for an appointment. It was

an appointment--one none of us expected—an appointment with death.

Debbie drowned trying to save her step-brother. She swam out to save him, and on her way back to shore with him, a current came and pulled them both under. They both drowned. That was in 1973. I was so sad, and sad for a long, long time. It took me years to stop grieving. I still miss her, though.

Chapter 2 – Home

New Home

Mama had gotten married in 1971 to Robert E. Portis, the man that would rear me until I left New Orleans, my home. To me, Robert was Daddy.

> *"When you are secure in your relationship with the Lord, then you will not be moved by the approval or disdain of others."*
>
> *Anonymous*

I learned later in life that my biological father is William Elmo Paye. A man who was an entrepreneur and owned a resale shop in Washington, D.C., which is where I was born. However, Mama moved back to New Orleans.

Our family moved into a predominately white neighborhood in 1974. It had only been 10 years since the Civil Rights Acts Movement passed in 1964. At the tender age of 7, I can recall how mean and hateful two of my white women teachers acted towards me. Fortunately, at the same time, I also had two very nice black female teachers that left a kind and memorable impression on me.

Some of the white families did not receive or welcome us into the neighborhood. One time, they egged the house and on another occasion they tried to set the house on fire, while we were in it!

I just happened to be leaving the den one night headed towards the bedroom when I noticed an orange flame outside the glass window next to the front door. Some of the neighborhood boys lit paper bags and threw them by our door. Boy, oh boy! My daddy was not happy with that situation! He was old school, and an ole' country boy from Alabama. You know the drill, go inside, get your rifle and protect your family! Of course, Mama was trying to calm him down and just get the police involved, which she did.

Some of these same young men used to spit at me and my sister out of the school bus windows. Just, plain ole' mean-spirited people. It was hard to comprehend this type of behavior, because I had not been taught to hate other people. Eventually, things changed for the better. We stuck through the hard times, though, and never moved away from the neighborhood.

> *"What we do not understand we have no right to judge."*
>
> *Henri Frederic Amiel*

For some strange reason, fifth grade was a game changer for me. I started getting in trouble in school, hanging out with the wrong crowd, fighting, etc. One day, my friends and I had gone to the principal's office one time too many.

My principal told us "If you girls come in here 'one more time,' you will be suspended, for three days!"

Well, since I knew who my Mother was, I never made it back to Ms. Garcia's office. One warning was enough for me! Don't have to tell me twice!

Home Away From Home

My sister and I often spent the night over to Aunt Lavonne's house. We had lots of friends that we had known since we were young. And, we would go over to my aunt's house a lot of times for the holidays. She always bought us the metal roller skates, the one with the key, for Christmas. You have to be a certain age to know what I'm talking about. I loved those roller skates. With the key, the skates became multiple sizes, worn over any closed-toed shoes. The key loosened nuts to widen the metal clamps on top and one to make them longer or shorter. The perfect gift for a young girl to share with friends, cousins and even siblings.

We had special friends, and I had one special friend in particular. I didn't realize how special until I became a teenager. As a young boy, he would throw rocks at me and run away and laugh. He was being a silly boy. At that time, he didn't know how to express his feelings for me. He was a very special friend whom I loved and cared for deeply.

Somehow, we lost touch with each other.

He was my childhood sweetheart. He felt the same way—an unspoken thing, yet very much understood. We always felt we were each other's true soulmate. However, by losing touch, I ended up marrying someone else. Later, we became life-long friends.

Chapter 3 – Growing Up

Jr. High School – 8th Grade

> *"When you dance to your own rhythm, people may not understand you; they may even hate you, but mostly, they'll wish they had the courage to do the same."*
>
> *Anonymous*

I fell in love with English, mastered the art of diagramming sentences, was great at spelling and received a trophy. I was awarded the trophy for having made all "A's" the entire school year. I was soooo excited!

Age 13 – Professed and Acknowledged Jesus as Lord and Savior

The most important day in my life was when I accepted Jesus Christ into my heart! Yes, even at the tender age of "13". Being as young as I was, I took a very strong interest in the Word of God. I began to read my Bible faithfully, and also began a prayer life. Something had changed inside of me. I felt new and different, pure and clean.

Ages 14-17 High School Days

Lots of fun, lots of learning, working jobs, and creating good memories. I was dating my high school sweetheart. We talked about getting married as soon as I finished school. Well, I made some bad decisions, and I did not adhere to some of the foundational principles I knew. I was a teenager in love. And as some teens do, experimented with kissing, hugging, caressing, and before long was caught up in the moment. I experienced two different types of love. Prior to the kissing and stuff, it was sincerely, philia (friendship), but then it turned to eros (sexual love). The next thing I knew, there was a baby on the way.

I refused to live otherwise with shame. Therefore, I became a young bride by the age of 17. I married the person who had become my high-school sweetheart. We simply married sooner than planned. Earlier, we talked about getting married as soon as I graduated high school, but obviously we got a little excited. I had some help in getting pregnant. It's not just the girl's fault you know. It was a team effort. That's my story, and I'm sticking with it. Ha!

> *"I would hate to die and never do the thing that I was born to do."*
>
> *T.D. Jakes*

However, I did graduate. In fact, I graduated number 70 out of 539 students. Not bad for a young mother-to-be. *And* I was nominated as "Most Likely to Succeed" by my classmates. I was the only female.

Our sisters were friends in school, and I was friends with his cousin that lived with him.

It just worked out that way! Surprisingly, to myself and others, I was seven months with child by the time I graduated from high school. Although I was married, I was not the first nor the last person to have this type of experience. Nor was I the only one expecting a child by our senior year.

Welcome To The Real World

Our first child was born in July, two months after graduation. My then husband, whom we will call Wade, chose to join the military and serve in the Air Force. After basic training, we made a decision to leave New Orleans to live approximately 80 miles away from home.

Chapter 4 – Predator in the Pulpit

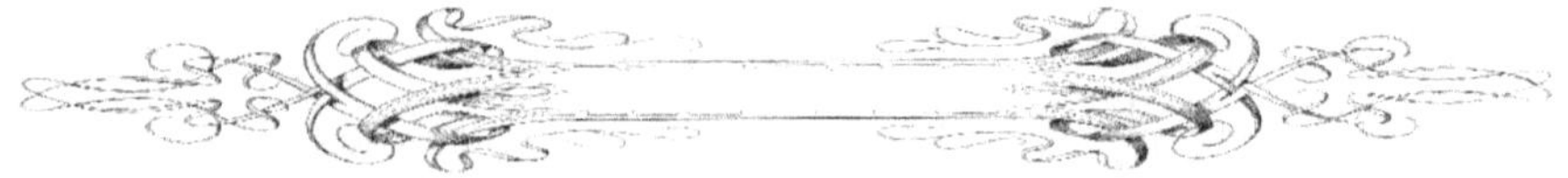

Life was good! Then we met the Browns. No pun intended to Tyler Perry's TV show Meet the Browns. We really did meet a couple with the last name Brown.

We met in our apartment complex and became very good friends. They invited us to church. The name of the church happened to be the same as my home church in New Orleans. The day we walked through the door, the minister that was up speaking caught my attention, and not in a good way!

> *"When people show you who they are believe them."*
>
> *Dr. Maya Angelou*

I remember clearly getting a very eerie feeling in the pit of my stomach, as I looked toward the pulpit. I did not share with anyone that I had a bad feeling, so we proceeded to go in.

We visited the church for a few months. In the meantime, the preacher that was standing in the pulpit when we walked in, had been in the process of starting his own church. Our new friends were very excited and decided to join him and persuaded us to go with them, so we did. Obviously, I ignored that gut feeling I had. The minister initially came across as sincere.

We started the church ministry in the home of this man

and his family. We had many Sunday services and weekday services. There was another couple that came with us too. Soon the church began to grow. We ended up finding a church building and moved the ministry from their family living room to a church sanctuary. Before long, numerous families had joined. A lot of the people were transient because of the military base.

Somehow, I ended up being the church secretary. I do not recall volunteering. I believe I was asked to serve in that role. What I do remember is what happened next.

One day, the minister wanted to discuss some church business. So, he asked Wade if he could drop by to review this information with me he needed typed up. That day came!

We discussed and reviewed whatever business it was that needed to be reviewed. Then, it happened!

He coaxed me from one end of the sofa to the other, persuading me to relax, to feel at ease, although, I was very far from that.

Pastor rubbed my shoulders and planted kisses on me. Not sure what to think or do, I froze internally. While he continued pressing himself against me, he tried to get me to relax, I couldn't. Suddenly, he had me beneath him. Like greased lightning, he unzipped his pants and then my clothes were undone. Shock took over as he used me for his pleasure. Suddenly I felt hurt, filthy, ashamed, exploited, and intimidated. I cried. I no longer felt like Ms. Goody Two-Shoes.

I was shattered . . . so shattered!

Just recalling that moment brings tears to my eyes, as I write. Mind you, I was still very young—only 19 years old, at this point. This person we all trusted and called Pastor or Minister Green was in his 40's.

> *"When we are hurting it does not give us a license to hurt others."*
>
> *Laura Schlessinger*

As days passed, there was unrest for my soul, unrest for my conscience. Yet, I was so very afraid to reveal to my husband at that time what transpired. I was afraid he would leave me. So, I buried the secret deep within!

"What else was a young bride to do?"

I was so afraid to speak up—afraid no one, not even those who loved me most--would believe my side of the story. I wondered if anyone would believe me.

Afterwards, Pastor asked for forgiveness and said, "I repent."

There were a couple of more meetings of coercion. Not all at our residence. By this time, I felt totally intimidated and exploited by way of fear. There was a lot of mental manipulation going on. I don't know how to explain this, but I was terrified, maybe even petrified. I almost felt indebted to this person. There were small favors done for my family, as if it were held over my head. I felt like I was under a spell. It was unwanted and unrequested sexual attention—more like relentless pressure. I didn't understand that I was experiencing sexual harassment back then. I just know the advances were unwelcome and unpleasant.

I should have spoken up. I should never have left it unspoken, letting fear keep me from revealing this terrible secret. This man of power intimidated me, but it wasn't just about me. I kept silent and left him free to do the same thing to anyone he chose.

Chapter 5 – The Winds of Change

Things began to change and transpire in the ministry that were just not right, not godly! To know and experience certain things firsthand got my attention. I realized I had compromised my integrity. Of course, hindsight is 20/20 vision, and experience is the best teacher. Sometimes when you are young, you don't always know the best way to handle a situation or the best thing to do. I didn't know how to go to someone and say, "Hey, there's a problem here!"

I regret not finding someone who could help me—someone I trusted enough to share what happened. If only one person said, "Speak up. Don't let this happen to you. Say something to somebody that can help you. Do NOT keep silent—no matter what that leader says." I believe I would have taken that advice.

Then one day, I noticed a very clear spirit of familiarity between Minister Green and another sister in the ministry – let's call her Charlotte.

At first, I kept it to myself. I tried to convince myself that maybe I only imagined it. Well, it happened more than one time after that. That's when I called Charlotte, because I considered her a friend at that point.

One day I took courage and asked "Is there something going on between you and Pastor Green?" In other words…"Are you in an intimate/sexual relationship with this man too?"

I explained to her what transpired on my end and how I felt about it.

I said to her, "This needs to stop!"

I felt used and abused because of his power and authority over me as my leader, as a pastor. But I felt somehow maybe with her help, we could challenge him as a united front. She made me think she agreed with me and that's what we would do!

> *"Whoever is careless with the truth in small matters cannot be trusted with important matters."*
>
> *Albert Einstein*

That did not turn out so great!

The next thing I knew there was a meeting between the three of us! She was furious with him and jealous! Charlotte was very angry! She also compromised her position and allowed her flesh to dominate over what was right. She told him I admitted what happened between us! She truly thought she was "the one" outside of his wife. Yes! He was also married, and so was my friend. We all were!

None of us were upholding the principles of Christ!

During the meeting, I told him the same thing I said to Charlotte. "This is not right! What you are doing is not right, and it needs to stop right now!"

Minister Green said, "I will not tolerate either one of you if you try to destroy my ministry or my name with this foolishness! No one will believe either of you."

Then he turned to me with much indignation. "It's none of your #@%& business what is going on between me and Charlotte, and if you tell anyone or if anything happens to this church it will be all your fault!"

"Ok, granted, but what about everything that happened between us?" I asked.

> *"The eyes of the Lord are in every place beholding the evil and the good."*
>
> *Proverbs 15:3*

"What everything? I don't remember any such thing. You say different, and it'll ruin you, not me. Everyone will believe you're a liar. You'd better not say anything like this in public."

I was to never say anything, "just hush!" That's how that was handled. And, so I did! I felt inferior to him.

His deep firm voice apparently became a powerful conditioning device. Had I become "brain-washed" unconsciously or was it more about thought control? He had a totalitarian attitude. He seemed to exercise control over my freedom of will and thoughts. In my mind, a complete authoritarian, bossy autocratic personality. At that time, I didn't realize I had been sexually, verbally and emotionally abused.

My conscience bothered me so bad. I could not bring myself to reveal to anyone else what was going on. I was truly afraid. I don't believe I ever experienced intimidation in my entire life up to this point. I became so introverted at times, it began to really bother me, and I held it in. But somehow I continued to function. I buried it! I hid it! I would not reveal what I was really going through! I wanted to tell my then husband so badly, but I didn't know how he would respond. I didn't know what he would say or do. I just couldn't take a chance, I couldn't bear the thought. I simply could not deal with it.

The other relationship continued while mine ended happily and swiftly, although I could not muster up the courage prior to that day. Charlotte could continue to live this way if she chose, but that was it for me! Eventually, a child was born from their relationship.

After a while, more people joined, the ministry continued to grow and God was saving souls and changing lives. This reminds me of the scripture in Philippians 1:15.

> ***"When it comes to faith, either you do, or you don't --- Believe."***
>
> *Arnita Ware*

"Some indeed preach Christ, even of envy and strife, and some also of goodwill...whether in pretense or in truth, Christ was still being preached." (NKJV)

The couple that encouraged us to join left.

In the meantime, other women experienced the same things, but nobody was coming forth. No one seemed to have the courage it took to stop this man! And obviously, there was an underlying motive, I suppose. I learned some things later and found out this man's background experience was similar in that he was a womanizer.

I can remember clearly, it was 1988, I can remember being with Minister Green one day running an errand for the church. I eventually volunteered my time working at the church office and the childcare center, many hours per day, but this particular day, we ran an errand to the post office. Mind you, I stuck to my decision that this man would not have his way with me ever again! That's how it was with me, but Charlotte had become obsessed, literally, with this man.

As we were walking, heading into the post office, I said

to Minister Green, "This is going to come out." It was as though the Lord was trying to warn him and give him a chance to get it right! And, I said it again, "I just have this strong feeling this is going to come out real soon!"

Well, little did I know, God was revealing it to another sister in the church--let's call her Sis. Fran.

Sis. Fran had begun having dreams and visions of what was transpiring in the church.

Here's the thing that really exposed this situation. There was a women's fellowship meeting at the home of one of the women of the church---we'll call her Sis. Sherrell. Pastor Green wanted to meet with the women for reasons I cannot recall right now. After everyone else left, this pastor asked her if he could use the shower, I guess under the pretense that he had another engagement. She allowed him to use it, but he had the gall to ask her to wash his back. Well, that decision broke everything wide open. What's more interesting is this woman had children living at home! So, it is not like she was "home alone" with him. In fact, she was a widow. She allowed him to use her guest restroom. What nerve Minister Green really had!

Sis. Sherrell then called and told what happened to another minister in the church—let's call him George Frier. Minister Frier had zero tolerance! Little did he know what had been transpiring right under his nose. He then insisted that he know everything. He wanted to know who knew what and this and that!

After this happened, one morning between 1:00 - 1:30 a.m., I received a call. My friend Charlotte was on the other end of the phone telling me her husband, George, knew what was going on.

The phone rang.

"Hello?" I answered with an attitude. Who dared call me in the middle of the night? This was prior to the days of caller ID.

Charlotte said, "Arnita . . . it happened!"

Half asleep, I mumbled into the phone. "Huh, what do you mean it happened? What happened? What are you talking about?"

"He knows!"

"Who knows? Charlotte, what are you talking about?"

She repeated herself, referring to George, who had just recently been told all the things that transpired.

And at this point, she began to confess the things she experienced with Pastor Green. So, you can imagine the havoc this must have created between her and her husband.

I sat straight up in my bed! "Oh, my God! I knew it! I knew this would happen! I knew it, I said it would happen, I had a strong feeling."

Of course, I was trying to whisper to keep from waking my then spouse, who was a pretty hard sleeper, but for some reason this particular night, he did not do so. I must have woken him up.

He began to question me. "Who are you talking to?"

"Charlotte."

It was not unusual for us to talk on the phone late at night, but she had never called at that time before. So, I told him, "I'll just go in the front." So, I did.

Eventually, I spoke to Minister George because he wanted to talk to me. "Nita, why did you not say anything to me?"

I considered him a big brother. He felt that as close as

we all were as couples, I should have felt comfortable in coming to him. And you know what? He was right! I should have! Shame filled my soul in the wee hours of that morning as tears trickled down my cheeks.

"I was afraid," I explained.

We began to talk, and I shared my version of what had been happening. Suddenly, Wade, entered the room wondering what was going on. Since, I was still on the phone, he figured it must be urgent. Of course, I did not want to say what was really happening and was taking place, but he could see the frantic look on my face.

I said, "Now I'm speaking to Minister Frier."

Wade snatched the phone from my hand.

Wade and I had been trying to have another baby, so I was seven months pregnant with our second child at the time of this incident. I didn't need any problems! Minister Frier told Wade the details of what he had just learned from Charlotte.

Wade furiously pointed at me and yelled, "Is that my baby?"

Being 100% certain, I said, "Yes!"

I can vividly remember the sick horrible feeling that I got at that time in the pit of my belly. I would have never expected to hear such a thing because I always knew. I never doubted, nor was it a question for me, because I had not allowed this man to be near me physically anymore, in an intimate way.

I knew I betrayed Wade's trust by not speaking up and standing for what was right. Indeed, I was afraid. But for him to suddenly hear of these things, left a big question in the back of his mind. So with all due respect, his anger and questioning was thoroughly understandable. Although I am not ordinarily the anxious type, this circumstance threw me for a loop.

Minister Frier reached out to Sis. Fran by phone. That's when everything all came to the light. The dots began to connect. Sis. Fran told Minister Frier of dreams and visions she had and how God revealed to her what was happening.

At Bible study, Wednesday, April 13, 1988, Sis. Fran asked if she could speak to the congregation. She said there was something on her heart she needed to share. At first, she was very reluctant to say anything to anyone.

Then she proceeded to say how while she was in prayer, a particular scripture laid heavily on her heart. She turned to Jeremiah 23:1-2 …"Woe to the shepherds who destroy and scatter the sheep of My pasture!" says the Lord. . . . "You have scattered My flock, driven them away and not attended to them. Behold, I will attend to you for the evil of your doings," says the Lord. (NKJV)

The room grew silent enough to hear a bug scuttle across the floor. No one knew exactly what it meant at that moment. She rebuked the minister for the things that took place .

Prior to church starting, Minister George and Charlotte tried to speak with Minister Green regarding the truth of what was going on, but he refused to confess or come clean and admit his faults. So, the chaos began!

There was a full--blown revelation. The truth was revealed in front of the congregation. Sis. Fran told of her dreams and visions, it exposed exactly what was happening. It was a God thing!

Wade who had been faithful in opening up the church

every Sunday and weekday service, exploded! I guess just the idea of hearing how bad the situation really was, made him even more upset. He was not normally one to say very much, but if he was upset, you knew it. He walked up to the pulpit, and slammed the keys to the church down on the podium.

He looked eye-to-eye with Pastor Green, and said, "You betrayed me! I trusted you! How could you do this? How could you do this to me?"

Wade turned around and walked away, looked at me and said, "Let's go!"

That's the last thing I recall at that exact moment.

Chapter 6 – After the Fallout: The Fellowship Dinner

After that night, suddenly I began feeling different. I couldn't seem to get the situation off of my mind. I was constantly thinking about it day and night. I kept thinking, "Oh, God, I can't believe this is happening, I'm so embarrassed!"

I didn't want anybody to know this, yet deep down inside, I really did. It raced through my mind. I kept thinking about it, and thinking about it, and thinking about it more, until I began having trouble sleeping. I heard voices, making me afraid to sleep.

I tried to fast and pray, attempting to deal with it as best I could. And then I became even more afraid.

I kept thinking, "I feel different. Something is happening to me!" I felt like I was changing, but I didn't really know what was happening.

For some reason, Wade and I went to Minister Green's house. I believe both of us were stressed at that point. We called to tell him we were on our way to his house. When we got there, the police were around. I lost control and tried to choke Minister Green right in front of the police officer.

After pulling me away, the office asked, "Do you want to press charges?"

"No. This isn't her usual character. Let her go."

We left and much of the following days and weeks remain blurred in my mind.

The next thing I clearly remember is having a fellowship at our apartment on Saturday, April 23, 1988. Some of our friends from the church were coming over. We all tried to stick together after the drama that happened at the church, not knowing what we were going to do next.

On the menu we had a big pot of New Orleans styled red beans and rice, fried chicken, and cornbread.

Mmmmm, mmmm! All my favorite foods. I also baked a cake. That night was the beginning.

Chapter 7 – My First Episode

I want to share this with you before I tell you what happened next.

If you would allow me to use and insert my artistic license here, I want to re-characterize the beginning of a Bible story in the book of Job, but substituting my name in place of Job. Job 1:1 & 1:6-12

"There was a woman in the land of America whose name was "Arnita"; and that young woman was blameless and upright and one who feared God and shunned evil".... (especially prior to this horrible experience).

Now there was a day when the daughters of God came to present themselves before the Lord, and Satan also came among them. And the Lord said to Satan, "From where do you come?" So Satan answered the Lord and said, "From going to and fro on the earth, and from walking back and forth on it."

Then the Lord said to Satan, "Have you considered My servant Arnita, that there is none like her, on the earth, a blameless and upright young woman, one who fears God and shuns evil?"

So Satan answered the Lord and said, "Does Arnita fear God for nothing? Have You not made a hedge around her, around her household, and around all that she has on every side? You have blessed the work of her hands, and her possessions have increased in the land. "

But now, stretch out Your hand and touch all that she has, and she will surely curse You to Your face!"

And the Lord said to Satan, "Behold all that she has in in your power, only do not lay a hand on her person." (In other words, don't take her life.) *So Satan went out from the presence of the Lord.*

In the true Bible version of this story several unfortunate things happened to Job soon after this interchange between God and Satan.

Job 2:1-6

Again there was a day when the daughters of God came to present themselves before the Lord, and Satan came also among them to present himself before the Lord.

And the Lord said to Satan, "From where do you come?"

So Satan answered the Lord and said, "From going to and fro on the earth, and from walking back and forth on it."

Then the Lord said to Satan, "Have you considered My servant Arnita, that there is none like her, on the earth, a blameless and upright young woman, one who fears God and shuns evil? And still she holds fast to her integrity, although you have incited Me against her to destroy her without cause."

So, Satan answered the Lord and said, "Mind for mind! Yes, all that a woman has she will give for her life. But stretch out Your hand now, and touch her mind and she will surely curse You to Your face!"

"Behold, she is in your hand, **but spare her life***." So, Satan went out from the presence of the Lord and struck Arnita in her mind.*

Satan had to have permission to attack me!

Chapter 8 – The Episode

What happened next?

On the night of the get-together, I wanted everything to be perfect. After a while, it got close to the time for the guests to come. In fact, the Brown's had already arrived. I excused myself to go bathe. It seemed to Wade that I was taking an extra-long time.

He knocked on the door and asked, "Honey, how much longer are you going to be?"

Snappily I replied, "Well, I can't decide what I'm going to wear."

"Well , Honey, you need to decide on something because the people are already here. The guests are already coming," Wade mumbled through the door.

> *"Don't compare your life to others. You have no idea what their journey is all about."*
>
> *Anonymous*

I just could not get it together that day. It took me an extra-long time to get dressed. I tried this outfit and that outfit, and I was not satisfied, because I could not figure out what to wear.

Confusion engulfed me. I couldn't remember how to get dressed, or the order in which I did things (methodically). I eventually got dressed and came out of the room.

Reggie asked me if I was okay.

I snapped at him too. "Yes, I'm fine!"

Trust me, I was not okay, nor was I fine! I had no clue that I was not okay, though. Again, I remember feeling strange and different, and acting strange and different, but I didn't know how to say, "I think something is wrong with me! I simply did not know how to express that!

And, even worse, I didn't even know my name!

For some reason, Reggie realized something was seriously wrong with me. He didn't know what was wrong, though.

He pulled Wade aside. "Hey Brother, something is wrong with Arnita!"

When Reggie noticed I was acting peculiar, he said, "Why don't we go down here to the room and let me talk to you for a minute."

Perplexed and quiet, I walked down the hallway toward my bedroom. I walked slowly, wishing I could run away instead of facing Reggie. He did not want to ask in front of everyone else.

Safe in the bedroom, he asked again, "Are you sure you are okay?"

"Yeah, I'm fine!" Even in answering, I snapped at him again.

Reggie asked, "What is your name?"

I sat for a minute before answering. "I don't know."

He asked again, "What is your name?"

Reggie knew me pretty well, so his voice and tone dropped down deeper. It was with more authority when he asked that time. He did not see or recognize the person that he knew standing in front of him.

When I did answer the question, I told him, "I'm Betty C. Green!"

Reggie grew agitated. "That is not your name! What is *your* name?"

"I don't know." I buried my head in my hands. "I don't know my name!"

And, I didn't! I had forgotten my own name. How do you explain to people that you don't know your own name? How do you explain to people that you are seeing things? How do you explain to people you are hearing voices in your head?

How can anyone understand that you are hearing the preacher's voice? And he is telling you he is going to come and get you and kill you. You are seeing his "green" eyes at night as they are coming toward you, in the dark!

Days prior to this dinner, I stopped eating and I stopped sleeping. Days had gone by, and I hadn't slept because in my mind I was fasting and praying.

I was slipping away mentally, and I didn't know it. I had no clue what was really happening to me. I didn't know I was sick.

I didn't know!

I do remember some of the guest began to leave, us canceling dinner for obvious reasons.

Apparently, I suffered a nervous breakdown behind all of this drama. What an experience. I lost my focus, my eyes somehow being taken off of Christ.

Some guest were leaving while others were arriving.

Bro. Reggie said to Wade, "We need to pray now. Something is wrong with your wife!"

So, those that were closet to me stayed and prayed with me.

I'm not sure if this happened the same night or not, but

I had a particular experience I remember and want to share.

For some reason, I was lying on the floor. Wade was on the phone talking to someone. All I know is that I remember thinking I was one of the two prophets lying in the street that the book of Revelation talks about.

The story takes place between the following chapter and verses: Revelation 11:1-19. I will use a portion of these verses to paint a picture of what I was visualizing.

Surely, I was hallucinating.

"And I will give power to my two witnesses, and they will prophesy one thousand two hundred and sixty days, clothed in sackcloth." (Rev. 11:3 – NKJV)

"And their dead bodies will lie in the street of the great city which spiritually is called Sodom and Egypt, where also our Lord was crucified. Then those from the peoples, tribes, and tongues, and nations will see their dead bodies three-and-a-half days, and not allow their dead bodies to be put into graves."

"And those who dwell on the earth will rejoice over them, make merry, and send gifts to one another, because these two prophets tormented those who dwell on the earth."

"Now after three-and-a-half days the breath of life from God entered them, and they stood on their feet, and great fear fell on those who saw them."

"And they heard a loud voice from heaven saying to them, "Come up here." And they ascended to heaven in a cloud, and their enemies saw them."

"In the same hour, there was a great earthquake, and a tenth of the city fell. In the earthquake seven thousand people were killed, and the rest were afraid and gave glory to the God of heaven."

"The second woe is past. Behold, the third woe is coming quickly."

"Then the seventh angel sounded: And there were loud voices in heaven, saying 'The kingdoms of this world have become the kingdoms of our Lord and of His Christ, and He shall reign forever and ever.'" (Rev. 11:8-15)

On another day, I had a similar biblical experience. Although, I was hallucinating, it all seemed so very real.

One day I was sitting in my living room on the love seat watching the news. Here's what I thought the news was reporting at that time.

The news anchor said, "Today we are reporting on what we think is known in the Christian church, as the "rapture". Today we saw planes falling out of the sky and crashing into the ground, and cars were clashing into one another. We saw people disappear! They simply vanished into thin air. We saw graves opening up and people ascending up in the air. We saw Christ hanging midair in the clouds." What they didn't mention is that they were left behind.

They had seen these things happening and they were wondering if this is really what the bible was talking about all this time. (The story is in I Thessalonians 4:13-18.)

I will focus on Verses 16-17.

For the Lord Himself will descend from heaven with a shout, with the voice of an archangel, and with the trumpet of God. And the dead in Christ will rise first. Then we who are alive and remain shall be caught up together with them in the clouds to meet the Lord in the air, And thus we shall always be with the Lord. I Thess. 4:16-17 (NKJV).

The next thing I remember is lying in my bed on my

back. When I opened my eyes, all these people were around my bed praying for me.

Days passed and some of the ladies from the church came over to assist me, since things were no longer the norm with me. Other people had to give me a bath.

I was only 20 years old, yet I had a nervous breakdown.

The stress of this embarrassing situation sent me completely over the edge. They told me I was very violent during that time, ripping and tearing people's clothes. Normally, I wouldn't harm a fly, well sort of. I hate flies! What's more interesting is that some parts of these moments, I can remember and other parts I can't. I continued having issues sleeping. Fear consumed me, and I seriously hallucinated.

For those of you who know what a tape recorder is, I'd like to describe what was going through my mind. You know what it sounds like when you hold the rewind or fast forward button down? That's how fast my brain was operating. I thought the man with the green eyes was coming to kill me. After all, he had said if anything happened to the church it would be all my fault. I drifted in and out of consciousness.

I believe I was at our apartment for approximately two weeks. Wade became afraid of me. I was a "mad woman," fearful at night. Wade was trying to figure things out on his own. Two weeks passed before he contacted my family.

Believe it or not, at that time, I did not know what the word "nervous breakdown" really meant. I heard the terminology before but did not have a true understanding, not at the age of 20. I didn't realize it meant losing your mind. Trust me, if I really knew what it meant, I would have certainly called my mother and said, "Mama, I'm sick.

Something is wrong with me. Please come and get me."

The next time, I was in the bed. My mother and Aunt Lavonne were there with me.

I recall waking up and saying to my mother, "Mama, what are you doing here? What are y'all doing?"

All these people surrounded my bed, or at least it appeared to be a lot of people. In reality, it was my mother, my aunt, Wade and some of the ladies from the church.

Then I asked Mama, "What's the matter with me, am I dying or something?"

She looked at me with her soft, deep dark brown compassionate eyes, and said, "No baby, you're not dying. You're just not feeling well right now."

So, I asked more specifically, "What's wrong with me?"

Mama said, "I don't know, but get you some rest."

That's all I can remember from that particular day.

Prior to my mother coming, I was at a point where I was basically incapacitated. I was not in my right state of mind and very pregnant. I was in no condition to take care of myself. So again, some of the ladies from the church came to help take care of me.

They made sure I ate. They had to bathe me and did everything they could to assist during this crisis. I never imagined someone having to do such things for me, and especially not at such a very young age. That's why we should be careful how we treat people, because we never know how we may end up and who's going to have to help you do what. You never know when you might need people.

During the time my mother and aunt were there, my youngest sister, whom we will call Ruby, was only 13 years old. She was also there.

I recall walking toward my kitchen and my sister was sitting on the floor in the corner by my trash can in a protective fetal like position. Her legs were drawn up toward her chest as she wrapped her arms around her own self, for protection.

Aunt Lavonne looked at her and asked, "What's wrong, baby? What's the matter?"

I was looking directly at her, but didn't realize I was the problem. As I write this story, it has been 30 years since these events took place in my life. My eyes still tear up every time I think about this.

She replied, "I'm scared of my sister! I don't like to see my sister like that!" Tears filled her eyes. "What's wrong with my sister?"

In spite of the fact I could not control myself, her reaction really touched my heart. To this day, I still remember the scene because I know it affected her greatly. She has always been precious to me. It affected me too, deep down inside, but there was nothing I could do.

I also remember talking to my older sister, who lived in Washington, D.C. Let's call her Arienne. We were on the phone one day, and she asked, "How are you?"

I responded, "Meow," just like a little kitten.

Poor Arienne. I learned later that while I was having a breakdown, so was her nearby best friend. She had a "double whammy"

Days would come and go. It was really strange. Believe it or not, during all of this turmoil going on in my mind, for some reason, I can recall some of the things I was doing. It was as if I were on the outside of myself looking in. I could see myself doing the things that were happening to me.

Don't ask me how, I cannot explain it. Somebody might call it an outer body experience. I don't know what you call it, but all I know is that it is as though I was watching a movie. But I was the main character in the movie.

That's the best way I can explain it.

I clearly remember one night. What appeared to be a very tall white figure stood at the end of my bed. It had wings, and I know it was an angel guarding me. I remember trying to sit up in my bed to touch it and see if it was real, but he moved backwards.

I don't know how long it was before I actually made it to a hospital. I was violent, strong, and totally out of character. I'm told I was taken to a mental facility in the state of Mississippi. Mind you, I was seven months pregnant. They told me it was a miracle that I was somehow released that day, because they were going to transfer me somewhere else, far away. It would have been almost next to impossible to see me on a regular basis. Thank God for the little miracles.

Since we lived near the military base and Wade was military, they did not have the proper facility for a person in my delicate condition. So, my parents came to get me where they could keep a close eye on me at a hospital in New Orleans. They also helped take care of my oldest son, who was almost three years old at that time. Mama had been taking him to the childcare across the street from the school where she worked. Before she would come and visit me, she'd take him to the house with Daddy. He would look after him while she visited me at the hospital. This was in April of 1988. So, I was in the hospital in New Orleans.

The devil tried to wipe me out, but God said "Not so!

It's not time!"

I tell you I was almost dead. I had stopped eating, sleeping, and I had a big black ring around my eye. I thought Wade hit me, although he never did that before.

I remember asking my aunt a question. "Aunt Lavonne, Did Wade hit me in my eye?"

"No, baby. It's because you have not been sleeping."

I was very dehydrated. My family had to rush me to the hospital to get nutrients in my system for the sake of the baby, and because I refused to eat. They had to treat me like a two-year-old child, except, I was 20. They had to force me to eat. I was "2" with a "0" behind it.

Chapter 9 – My Hospital Rooms

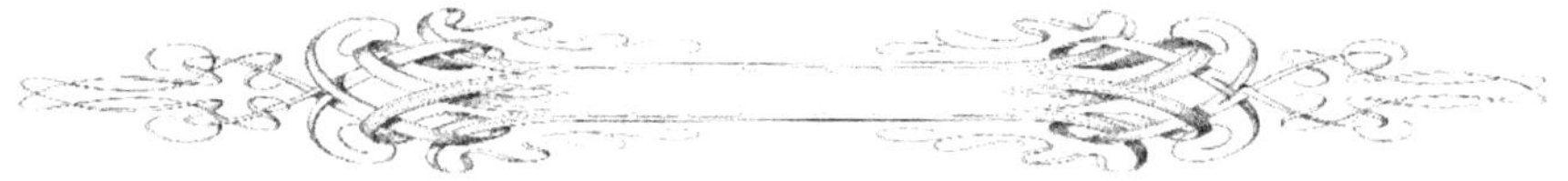

Before going to Southern Baptist, I was admitted to another hospital called DePaul.

Suddenly, I became violent again, and it began to be a danger for the baby. I could have hurt my baby, myself, and anyone else that was near.

I clearly recall being in a padded room, the walls cushioned with whatever protective covering it was. And I recall being in a strait jacket. I leaned against the wall—a dull, boring gray wall.

I hated it.

The wall looked very boring to me. I hate blank walls anyway, and the gray color made it worse.

I recall thinking, "Why am I here, where is everybody?"

A small square window in the steel door allowed me to peep out, but limited my vision to only a small section of hallway.

"I'm scared, where is everybody?"

I remember how uncomfortable I felt in this room. I didn't understand why I was there. During this stay, it was one of those times I could see myself in the strait jacket walking around the room and leaning on the wall. I could see myself lying on the table. But somehow, I managed to get ***out*** of the wrist bands they used to strap me to the table.

Then they relocated me to Southern Baptist Hospital on Napoleon St. One night, when I was no longer wearing restraints, I was jumping up and down on the bed pushing the ceiling tiles. I don't know if I thought I was on a trampoline, or what. That was enough for me to fall off the bed and injure myself, and in the process, lose my precious baby. I was certainly not in my right mind at all.

Yet, I realize God was with me all the time. Even in the confusion of my mind, He remained right there.

I still experienced sleeping issues. I will ***never*** forget my room. Darkness filled me with sheer terror. Paranoia screamed at me in the night hours. Of course there was a set time to go to bed. I did not have the liberty of watching T.V. when I couldn't sleep.

I could see the street lights shining into my room. Although I was afraid to sleep, the only thing I could think was his eye (God's eye) is on the sparrow and I know he's watching over me.

In fact, it was as if the scriptures had been ***totally erased from my brain.*** I couldn't even remember the 23rd Psalm. All I could recall was, "The Lord is my shepherd and I shall not want."

That's it! That was ***all*** I could recall. Like ***abracadabra***, it seemed to have vanished. I mean I had been a Bible scholar. Can you imagine that? I knew the Word of God because I read my Bible all the time. Even though that is all I ***could*** remember, I thank God because The Lord is my Shepherd and, I shall not want. This really made a difference for me.

I determined, if this was all I knew, that's exactly what I was going to say over and over to myself.

Some nights I drifted off to sleep, and some nights I didn't. In the meantime, the doctor tried to balance my medicine where I could sleep and try to get well enough to go home by the time I had the baby.

Several times the hospital thought they would be able to release me to go home. But the closer I got to going home, the more I acted out. Either the medicine was too strong or too weak. It was simply unbearable.

For some strange reason, during all of this "madness," I suddenly developed a hatred towards my mother and Wade, the two people closest to me, that I loved most. Mentally, I reverted back to my childhood. Something happened to me, I had changed. I was not the nice girl everyone knew. I had been under attack, and my brain simply couldn't handle the stress of it.

I refused to eat. I did not feel hungry. I was dehydrated. At one point I had to have an IV. However, the hospital provided Ensure for me to drink, as well. Sometimes it was breakfast, lunch, and dinner because I would throw my food at them. I didn't want it, I didn't want to be bothered with anyone during this time.

In my seventh month of pregnancy, everyone did their best to get me to eat and drink. Whenever my mother visited, we played a game called "red light" before I would eat.

I would say, "One, two, three, red light!"

That meant I had to stop eating.

Mama would say, "Nita, I need you to eat your food. You need to eat for the baby."

I would say to her, "But you didn't say 'Go'."

So, she would answer, "Mama says go!"

Then I would open my mouth like a little baby and eat.

> *"For He shall give his angels charge over you, to keep you in all thy ways."*
>
> *Psalm 91:11 (NKJV)*

There was a nurse whom I truly believed was my deceased cousin, disguised as an angel. She looked so much like her. There was another lady I believed was my grandmother, although I never laid eyes on her. She passed away when I was two years old. Perhaps they were my guardian angels while I was in the hospital in that warped state of mind.

It was awful. I was locked up, and I couldn't get out!

There was a very small patio that we were periodically allowed to go out on every once in a while. Talk about enjoy your freedom and don't take things for granted. I learned my lesson way back then.

In the midst of all of this, came some humor I can look back upon and still laugh to this day. On one of the nights that I watched T.V. the movie *Rocky*, with Sylvester Stallone, was on. I've always enjoyed this movie. For some reason, which I still cannot recall how, before the movie was over, I managed to get ahold of a roll of gauze.

I wrapped up both of my hands, as if I was getting ready for a full blown boxing match. I remember being in the middle of the hallway juggling side to side, and back and forth like a boxer does as they are getting ready to hit their opponent.

I don't recall seeing anyone visually in front of me, but perhaps I was just getting some practice in. Perhaps I was preparing to fight the "negative force" that was trying to wipe me out—the Devil.

One of the nurses who was already laughing, spotted me in the middle of my imaginary act and asked, "What are you doing?"

"I'm boxing! What does it look like I'm doing?" I answered. "My name is Rocky."

By this time, I knew my real name. I was just clowning around.

Chuckling all the way toward me, she helped me get unraveled so I could get ready for bed, which was coming up shortly after the movie went off. This was a sign I was getting better, because I had to laugh at myself too. She couldn't wait to tell my mother the next day when she came to visit.

Yes, it is funny to me too, every time I think about that night, even to this day; I still laugh.

I was a big-bellied seven-month pregnant woman ***boxing.*** *Ummph! Ummph! Ummph! SMH (Shaking my head)!*

One day my daddy came to visit me, and I got all excited because I just knew he was coming to take me home. I did not go home that day and was terribly disappointed.

Eventually, my condition got better. I was eating and sleeping like I should. I worked my way up to getting weekend passes to be at home with my family. My parent's home was as far as I was allowed to go, and then back to the hospital. I was not mentally stable enough to go anywhere else. My mother came to see me every single day for two months except one day when it was storming. She asked to speak to me by phone to tell me she was not going to make it, but I wouldn't have wanted her to drive in such stormy weather.

Wade also came to see me ***every*** single weekend.

I was hospitalized from April through June of 1988. On one of my weekend passes home, I went into labor. I was awakened, straight up out of my sleep when a labor pain hit me in my lower back at 12:15 a.m. We rushed to the hospital. I managed to convince my mother to come into the delivery room with us. I had my second baby boy three hours later, June 5th. Thankfully, the meds I was on did not affect my baby. Thank God he was okay.

I was released from the hospital five days after that. I stayed at my mother's house a few more weeks after the baby was born, just to make sure I was stable before going back to Mississippi.

My psychiatrist, who we will call Dr. Steward, was a much older, refined gentleman. He is the person I began seeing while I was still in New Orleans.

He asked, "Do you remember why you went to the hospital? What happened to get you to this point?"

He was so nice. "You're the youngest patient that I have ever had. And I've certainly never heard of a person able to recall some of the incidents they have been through."

He looked at my mother and asked, "Do you all have a history of mental illness in your family?"

Mama answered, "Not to my knowledge."

He asked various questions, and I answered all I could remember.

At that time, he diagnosed me with acute schizophrenia. I went to see him for a few follow up visits before I went back home with Wade.

Eventually, I went home to Biloxi, which really took some adjusting after being hospitalized for two months. It took me a while to become comfortable again being in a home environment, no restraints. I could get up when I got ready. I could walk around when I got ready. Total freedom. It felt weird! I wasn't imprisoned any longer. So, in my mind, that took a huge adjustment, as well as trying to take care of a newborn baby when I was not exactly totally well myself. But I was well enough to be released from this mental institution.

After returning home and adjusting, I began to go back around friends who had been around me and saw me when I was ill. It was very difficult for me at first. They had been asking about me, but now I had to face them. I knew they loved me, but that was not really the question. It was a matter of me again becoming comfortable being in their presence, especially knowing what I had been through.

"What are they saying about me?" I wondered. "Do they think I'm crazy? Are they afraid of me, like Wade?" I knew this was new to him too.

A part of me was embarrassed, yet I had no control of the situation that happened to me. One thing I learned, even all these years later, is that we have to accept what God allows. And I realize God was and is still sovereignly in control of my life--even at that time, no matter what the situation appeared to be.

As time went on, I continued to take my medication. The medication and visits continued back on the military base. I was like a zombie. I did not like the way the medicine made me act and feel.

The doctor's questions were routine. "Who is the

President of the United States?"

"President Ronald Reagan."

"Do you have thoughts of suicide?" She jotted down notes. "How do you feel today?"

I answered the questions correctly, showing signs of becoming myself again.

Time went on, and I continued to take the medication, trying to take it as consistently as possible.

But then as months passed, there came a day when I began to feel like I didn't really want to take this medicine anymore. Each follow up visit resulted in the same ole' humdrum, repetitive questions.

"Do you know today's date?"

"Yes."

"What is your name?"

"Arnita."

"Do you have thoughts of killing anyone?"

"No, of course not."

"Do you have thoughts of killing yourself?"

"No."

At some point, I told Dr. Laymon, "I am going to stop taking the meds!" Gradually, I did.

Before this happened though, once or twice I tried to go cold turkey, but would start getting sick, because my body had gotten used to the medicine. So, I would start back taking it.

Chapter 10 – A Simple Meal

I was at home one day attempting to cook my favorite meal, spaghetti and meatballs. As I was making the meatballs, I was unable to roll a round meatball, although I had made them a thousand times.

They appeared to come out square or flat. That was not going to cut it for me.

I looked over at Wade who was helping in the kitchen and said, "Honey, can you help me? I can't do this!"

He looked at me, surprised, and said, "Honey look at you. Now as many times as you've made this (not in a critical tone, but in a way to capture my attention). It goes like this."

Wade took the ground meat from my hand and began to make the meatball in his hand. Then he put some ground meat in my hand, and as I proceeded to roll it, he put his hand on top of mine and rolled my hand in a circular motion to create a meatball.

"See, it goes like this."

And I tell you, while he was helping me roll that meatball, the light came on (in my mind). I felt like God had just revealed something to me. That's when I knew I did not want to be in this condition for the rest of my life.

You might be thinking, "You're already out of the hospital. What condition are you talking about?"

Rolling those meatballs made a difference. I was like a zombie. I was not the energetic, enthusiastic person I was before the breakdown or that I am today. I had become slow in everything. I talked slow, moved slow, and even thought slowly.

Everything had seriously changed! I became the opposite of everything I ever was naturally.

That's when it registered—that's when it hit me.

"I don't want to be like this the rest of my life, I can't be like this the rest of my life!"

I made a conscious and spiritual decision that I really needed God's help to keep me from being on this medication for the rest of my life. I felt I was too young to be what I called "handicapped." I truly felt incapacitated.

I said, "God, if you made me, certainly, you can heal me!"

Again, I reiterated my plans of stopping the meds to the doctor.

She liked to have had a conniption fit. "Oh, no! Please don't do that! It is not a good idea to stop taking your meds. It is a high possibility that you could have another breakdown."

In fact, she even mentioned that I should at least be on the medication for up to one year, if not for the rest of my life.

"But you don't understand. I do not want to be on medication for the rest of my life, and I'm going to stop taking this medicine.

She reaffirmed her professional opinion. "Please don't do this!"

But she didn't understand what I was saying. I couldn't be on this medicine for the rest of my life.

So, I gradually decreased myself from the medicine. I would lessen the dosages. I can't even remember how much I was supposed to take each day, but I did decrease the medicine daily, and it seemed to be working.

Well, I took my chances. I stopped the meds. (Do not try this at home!) Next thing I knew, all of a sudden, I was "cold turkey." I had stopped taking the meds altogether. I was just fine. I can't tell you which day I got better, or when I got better. I just know I was back to myself again.

Fifteen months later, I gave birth to a third son. Prior to giving birth, I entered business school and took a 600-hour comprehensive secretarial course. I didn't know I was expecting my third child when I enrolled. However, the course was from February to September 1989. I ended up not graduating with my class (crossing the stage) because my son was born two weeks early on September 4th. Of course, I still received my certificate.

My oldest son turned four on July 18th and had two little brothers. He loved being a big brother.

> *"We all stumble and fall at times, but the only real failure is in staying down. Victory comes when we stand up and move forward again"*
>
> *Anonymous*

We ended up moving—from Mississippi to Texas where "everything is bigger."

Before moving, I prayed sincerely about a new church home, because I had just recovered from a very bad experience. God led us to the right church where I have been a member since 1990.

Lo and behold, there were other experiences throughout the relationship where now both parties had been unfaithful to each other. Total transgressions, one against the other. I must say, there were a few relational crisis, yet it did not excuse what we had done. I will say this, for the selfish and selfless times that I was inclined to go along at my discretion, I truly regret. It's never worth hurting someone else, no matter how gratifying it may seem at the moment one is caught up. I have wondered at times if I was somehow acting out from the previous abuse. We went through periods of learning how to trust again, learning to forgive, because we so desperately wanted to keep our family together. So, as time passed, we matured and began to help other couples.

People admired us, and called us "The Perfect Couple." We even began a marriage ministry and sometimes, we had several couples at a time. Wade and I would attend marriage conferences annually. I was always admitting to other couples that we had been through rough patches in our relationship so others could understand it is possible to move forward, if you choose to forgive and try again. I even shared publicly whenever I would minister. (Yes, by the way, I have a calling on my life. I remember when I heard that still small voice speaking clearly to me, saying, "I have called you to ministry". I remember saying, "God, you can't be talking about me because I've done abc, xyz, and 123. I was completely restless in my spirit until I answered the call. So I was always clear with people that I am a perfect example of past failures. I've never tried to hide, so to speak.

At other times we used to just have food and fellowship with other couples from our church. Sometimes we had 5 to 10 couples at a time in our home. One couple we spent much more time with than others, because Wade and I are the godparents of one of their daughters, considering we had sons. I was so excited because I would have the opportunity to help rear and influence our little goddaughter. Although, I have another goddaughter, Wade is not the godfather.

Times were changing and we were growing closer, or so I thought. Next thing I knew, at some point, I started feeling a slight distance or strain in the relationship. Somehow, I could not exactly put my finger on the problem.

"It's a funny thing – you work all your life toward a certain goal, and then somebody moves the post on you."

> *"People change and forget to tell each other."*
>
> *Lillian Hellman*

Chapter 11 – When Things Fall Apart Beyond Belief

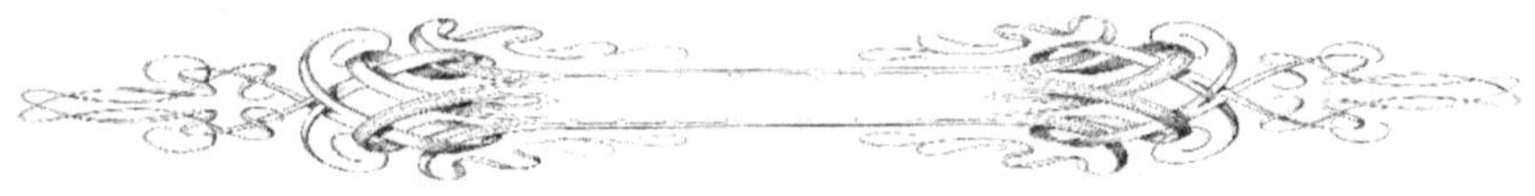

> *"Resilience is the ability to recover from or adjust easily to misfortune or change."*
>
> Merriam Webster

The following is a peek into a season of my life:

As if I had intruded upon a major event, there was a deafening silence. My house was absolutely quiet. As I walked in, I had a suspicious feeling that something was not quite right; something was awry.

Two weeks before our oldest son's high-school graduation, there was so much to do and such little time. As usual, I ran home on my lunch hour, although, one hour earlier than the norm. When I approached the house I thought I saw a silhouette pass the window, but I was uncertain. Could it be? To my surprise, the kind that knocks the wind out of you, I caught them. Alone, together, and absolutely unauthorized to be in their birthday suits.

Wade was unemployed at the time. I believed he was diligently "looking for a job." Well, perhaps he was in his own selfish way.

How could he have been so inconsiderate, ruthless, and despicable of his wife and children? How could he not consider that she was supposed to be a friend, considered as a sister? And her husband, who was his friend, was like as unto a brother. Not to mention, we were the godparents of one of their daughters, which tied our families together like blood relatives.

With that being said, it is clear to me there is a real reason for the phrase "crime of passion." In that moment, I stood there confronting her, with the expectation, of a legitimate reason as to why she was in my home naked, in the middle of the day. Although, no time was the right time. She stood there looking dumbfounded, as if I were speaking a foreign language.

Suddenly, she was thunderstruck, when I smacked the crap out of her face. Fortunately, her gasp for air somehow snapped me back into reality. I'm afraid if it were not for that, there would have been two funerals. Meanwhile, he stood there looking powerless, unable to comfort her, yet wanting to reach out and touch me.

I was not having a "Ma Bell" moment. Immediately, I pushed him into the wall, refusing personal contact from him—no desire for meaningless touch. To me, it was such a detestable act, not to mention, he was a man of the cloth.

In spite of the misfortune of ultimate betrayal, the episode was somehow compartmentalized, so, I managed to celebrate my son's accomplishments. He was graduating with honors as Magna Cum Laude, and I was proud as ever.

Although, this may be achievable, reconciliation seemed impossible. Empty promises to seek counseling led to the delay in filing for divorce after 20 invested years in marriage. Nonetheless, one year later, more of the truth was revealed. It felt like another level of betrayal. I know it would not have felt so painful if we were not all so close. Her husband lost it. We thought we were in a sister/brother type relationship, but somebody flipped the script.

As a result, this led to a fight at church. It was total public humiliation. More church drama--*again*? Now the whole world knew what was going on. We were all so deeply hurt, embarrassed and the whole nine yards. It was truly difficult to keep a sincere smile on my face. At that point, I filed for divorce.

In the middle of this incident, my father was dying of prostate cancer. Truly, it had to be my darkest hour. Once again, I had to compartmentalize, in order for me to honor my father's life and grieve properly over his demise. Consequently, I did not do well. I was physically at daddy's funeral, but not mentally. Had my mind reverted back to the six-year-old little girl at Debbie's funeral? Was I experiencing PTSD? I checked myself into a hospital, simply overwhelmed.

Incidentally, after all of this, I dropped the divorce for the sake of the children.

One day I somehow ended up talking to her by phone. I described my pain to her, in the best way I could. I said, "I would rather that you had taken a knife, looked me in my eyes, and stabbed me in my heart, because that is exactly what this pain feels like!"

I paused, and she remained silent. "From now on, every time you see me, think of me, or hear my name, you'd better thank God for your life!"

I truly realize that things could have gone bad, really bad, just like the dreams. Apparently, she did not understand the gravity of the situation. God truly helped me during that precise moment. Even though, I would have been within my rights, I'm just glad I do not have anyone's blood on my hands.

Eventually, I came to my senses. We never made it to

counseling, and he continued to make contact with her, blatantly lying and telling me the opposite of the truth.

One day, I looked in the mirror and said to myself, "You are better than this, and you deserve better!"

The real truth, in my heart I felt like he was really lying to me, I began to get more and more bitter. In my heart I started feeling like I wanted to kill him and I mean for real.

I shared this with a very close family friend who knew both of us very well.

He said, "Sis. Arnita, if that's how you are really feeling, then it's time to go!"

I know I am not a murderer. And besides, I had already dreamed twice that I caught him with another woman. But in my dreams, I could not see the face. Yet, in the dreams, I murdered them both. I shared this with Wade each time it happened. I thank God that He kept my mind from completely snapping, that awful day.

Even the woman that injured me so deeply, I had poured into her, investing precious time and love--years' worth. I shared my experiences with her, hoping she would use the wisdom I shared with her, and learn from my mistakes. I shared what to do and what not to do, and how not to live.

I said clearly, "It is not worth it to hurt other people."

Prior to accepting her friendship she pleaded for, I made it explicitly clear, "I deal with very few women!"

And, I asked her to please not take my friendship lightly or for granted. I loved her with the love of a younger sister. So much that I even offended my own little sister. For that to be taken lightly or for granted was very heart rending.

I'll never forget when she called me one day and asked, "Do you think it is possible to have a friendship with someone of the opposite sex and not be in a relationship with them?"

I replied, "Yes, it is possible, but it is a very fine line, and one has to be very careful."

Not one time did the thought cross my mind—she's stabbing me in the back or is going to. That's how much I trusted her. People of God, let us be mindful to be people who pray and not people who prey.

It has since made me want to put up walls when I meet new people. However, I realize that everyone is not out to harm me. All I know is I loved her like the love David and Jonathan had in the Bible.

In spite of everything, it's all good!

One thing I can say—others may try to imitate me, but they'll never be able to "duplicate" me! Ha! The mold was broken when I was born. I am a one of a kind lady. And you can take that to the bank! Ha! "Be the best you can be. There is nothing sadder than being a second-rate imitation of someone else." (Arnita Ware)

I simply refused to stay in a marriage where someone was physically there, but not mentally, emotionally, connected to me.

I told him, "If you want her that bad, then you can go move in the house with her and her husband." And I meant every word! I filed for divorce a second time, which was finalized two days before my 22nd Anniversary.

> *"Sometimes you have to know when to call it quits."*
>
> *Steve Roller*

Chapter 12 – 2005
Official Diagnosis of Bipolar Disorder

Once again, life dealt a big blow! ***Another nervous breakdown!***

21st century terminology, "melt down." Melt down, break down, out of my mind, call it what you want. If you had to walk in my shoes during all of this stress, you don't know how you would have ended up either. I was hospitalized for approximately two weeks after Daddy's funeral. Then I attended therapy sessions about a week later. Millwood Hospital has seen me quite a few times. It took me ***seven years*** to accept the reality of this diagnosis. I've discovered that "stress" is NOT my "best friend."

Millwood Hospital has a beautiful courtyard where patients can go outside primarily to smoke. But I liked being outdoors. From time-to-time, someone in the hallway would yell, "Smoke break." I quickly joined the smokers, but once outside, I ventured off to a corner of the courtyard. It gave me a spot to sit quietly and contemplate.

As I sat in that peaceful corner, the words to a song popular in the early 1970's came to mind. "God is so Good" rang through my head, the simple words reverberating in my confused mind. And soon the words came out, clear and strong. Suddenly everyone in the courtyard grew quiet as I kept singing.

Before long, when anyone headed out to the courtyard, they'd come looking for me and wait without a word for me to sing that simple little song again.

In the very midst of a messed-up, confused state of mind, God worked in and through me to comfort people who found themselves at Millwood Hospital at the same time I was there. It certainly wasn't me. I was in no condition to help myself, let alone anyone else. But God stood in that courtyard with me, using the very thing that comforted me to reach others as well.

There was a 17 year gap from 1988 to 2005, where I was episodeless--maybe. There may have been a time or two that I should have been hospitalized when I think about some of the circumstances going on in my life. But somehow, I ended up resting and sleeping it off for a few days.

I learned later that this is a genetic illness. It's somewhere in my genes. Altogether, I've been hospitalized six times in my adult life. This helped me to come to the realization that something was truly going on with me. What I have discovered is there are certain "triggers" that cause me to be hospitalized.

My most recent hospitalization was in 2016, at Arlington Memorial (Behaviorial Health). I attended five to six funerals within two months. Way too much for me.

The doctor said, "You are grief-stricken."

Once again, I believe I was traumatized when my cousin died. I probably needed counseling back then, but who did such things in the 70's? I don't think it was common knowledge that children can also have stress and/or triggers. And, now I have to be more selective in attending funeral services, particularly where there is a physical body.

When I was hospitalized one year in Dallas Presbyterian Hospital, a doctor told me "You have the intelligent man's disease." And then he said, "Bipolar disorder is a cross between "genius" and "madness."

> *"Forgiving those who hurt us is the key to personal peace."*
>
> *G. Weatherly*

I responded, "I choose the 'genius' side!"

So why am I revealing such a personal medical issue? Why should I air my dirty laundry?

I am 50 years old at the time I'm writing this book, and I'm old enough to own up to ALL of my issues and brave enough to share it with the world. Not in my own bravery, but because I've always known, I would end up being a testimony to other women, and ***people*** in general.

I am not "bipolar!" I suffer from bipolar disorder. People are simply, people.

I am ***so much more*** than the illness. I have so much more to offer the world. Granted, it truly makes me feel very complex and diverse at times. I really try not to be complicated.

Why is mental health not treated with respect and dignity?

I wish the world would "embrace" this illness as any other serious illness. Unfortunately, it is often ridiculed. I wish there were more social empathy, more mindfulness of mental health concerns, more awareness.

There were many moments when I struggled to simply leave the house, especially to attend church. Somehow, I convinced myself that no one would miss me. This illness can take you real low. It can make you feel very embarrassed, very demoralized, mostly because there is such a stigma concerning any mental illness. But this is how I feel. If people can get online and talk about all other illnesses, breast cancer, or MS, high blood pressure, lupus, or whatever, then, why can't I talk about my ***invisible*** "brain illness?"

You know, my oldest sister really helped me to come to the realization and acceptance of this illness, and in convincing me to take my medication.

She said, "Nita, you need to take your medicine. Just like people take medicine for diabetes, heart condition, blood pressure, or any other health concerns, you need to consistently take your medicine, too."

The other thing that really helped me to stick with taking the meds is that I realized I did not want to endanger my grandchildren, nor feel that I could not be trusted to care for them.

Someone might call me "special," "extra," "over the top," or "eccentric." Whatever the case, I am what I am. I am who I am, and it is what it is. I am who I am by the grace of God.

> *"What other people think of you is none of your business."*
>
> *Anonymous*

I finally accepted this illness for what it really is, genetic, treatable and manageable. So, I've decided to open up, shed the shame and embarrassment, speak up and speak out.

My brain is simply "wired" a different way. Bipolar disorder is simply a ***"medical condition,"*** not a definition of who I am.

I will say this, once I understood that I had bipolar disorder, then I began to understand why some things may have happened the way they did in my life. So, no, I am truly not proud of some of the things I've done, or the error of my ways during my lifetime. In fact, usually when I have an episode, I've done some rather embarrassing things or said and done things totally opposite of my natural character. My alter ego comes out. (A person's secondary or alternative personality) Not good. And I also know I have hurt people I love or loved, because of it.

The word bipolar means two extremes. Life is split between two different realities, elation and depression. It is a permanent non-curable mental illness.

I believe in the power of prayer, but God also gives us wisdom and has provided some healing by way of doctors and medication to stabilize people so they can live a successful life and function as they were meant to be. Most people with various mental illness conditions are extremely creative. Albert Einstein was one of them--a real genius.

I also want other people to know, "you are not alone." I've gone through these things. Yet, I came out victorious. I'm still standing. And, if I can make it, you can too. This story is not about being a victim, or pointing the finger, but simply to share my truth, my experiences.

It took me ***years*** to heal. To the degree that I had to temporarily separate myself from the things and people most familiar and dear to me. The pain was too great.

I realize people can get "caught up" in the moment. I get it. Been there, done that. It is very easy to get caught up in a situation that is bigger than you. So, I understand. It's a sex trap! Call it what it is.

Sex Trap.

Sex a universal word--a universal issue. People sometimes will not call a spade a spade. It's just that it hurts worse when you have committed the act against someone or if the act has been committed against you, ***especially*** in the church.

> *"Never be ashamed to own you have been in the wrong, 'tis but saying you are wiser today than you were yesterday."*
>
> *Jonathan Swift*

This is where it hurts the MOST, I'm convinced. Since, I have been on both sides of the fence, I can speak from both angles. Yet, in my heart of hearts, I love the Lord! At times I have felt like King David, a person after God's own heart, yet have failed many times. At least I felt like a failure to myself, to God, and those that I know I disappointed. However, I have done some things "right" in my lifetime. I often reflect on the book of Matthew the twenty-fifth chapter to remind me of what I ***should*** be doing. I thank God that he looked beyond my faults, and saw my needs.

So, let me ask you a question. What is your social identity? Who are you behind the scenes? "What will your legacy be?"

"Even if the grass is greener on the other side of the fence . . . the lawn still has to be mowed!"

Arnita Ware

Chapter 13 – Starting Over

Being Single

> "Expect trouble as an inevitable part of life, and when it comes, hold your head high. Look it squarely in the eye, and say, "I will be bigger than you. You cannot defeat me."
>
> Ann Landers

I couldn't believe it. There I was 39 years old and divorced after almost 22 years of marriage.

"What am I going to do?" I wondered.

I remember feeling scared. I had no problem entertaining myself, since I enjoyed reading, writing, painting, chatting with family or friends in my spare time.

But this would be different.

I would actually begin living ALONE for the first time in my life. Could I handle it? Would I enjoy it? Would I be afraid? What about the income? Can I afford my own place to live, my vehicle payment, and medical insurance on a microscopic salary?

Thank God for Mothers. My mother volunteered to assist me momentarily, until I could get back on my feet. Obviously, she understood that it felt as if a rug had just been yanked from under me. Perhaps, it was. Still somehow I knew I was truly on solid ground. It was the support of others, their prayers, and of course the eternal one, who carried me. The proof was the footprints in the sand.

Additional Income

I needed more money. Yes, I was grateful for what I already had, but I refused to live below my standard of living. Pride you might say--don't know if I would narrow it down to that. It was so much more. It was the fact I had children to be mindful of. I needed them to understand that even when life throws its toughest blows, you CAN make it. Do much more than what others expect of you.

Show yourself you are a survivor, is what I told myself.

Sometimes it was difficult to accept my experience, especially in the eyes of all who knew us as a couple, as well as the other couple involved. Needless to say, I began my search for additional work.

At first I ended up working part-time at an athletic club for a few weeks, and then I ended up working at a fashion store. I was a reliable cashier for approximately three years. It kept me busy and my mind off of my circumstances. I didn't have time to feel sorry for myself.

Liberated at 40

Several months after the divorce, I turned 40. Lordy, Lordy, look who's forty. Free at last. It felt like a weight was lifted. I felt great and definitely looked good. The stress had packed on a few extra pounds, but I lost about 20 pounds. I was happy. I was smiling again. I threw myself a 40th birthday dinner party. Sorry you missed it.

"Standing by faith, sometimes means standing alone."

Arnita Ware

Chapter 14 – Healing and Moving Forward

It Took Time to Heal

> *"Right is right, even if everyone is against it; and wrong is wrong, even if everyone is for it."*
>
> *William Penn*

After several years of wondering why, words simply cannot express the depths of pain and mental anguish this experience brought on. I somehow managed to hold my head up although my heart had been broken. I met this person at the tender age of 14 and married three years later. Yes, in spite of the fact I was a "child bride," I managed to keep a marriage of 21.9999 years.

I asked myself, "What went wrong?"

How did we get there? Was it lack of communication, lack of caring, was there no more love? Of course, I realize, neither of us had been saints in the relationship. I mean, I can truthfully admit, I was still emotionally attached to a childhood friend. So I cannot say perhaps this was not a factor which contributed to some of the problems in that relationship. But, to cross the lines with a woman I considered as a blood sister? That was a bit much.

So, after almost 22 years of marriage, life changed for me when my high-school sweetheart and I ended up divorcing after his infidelity with my supposedly very close friend. The vicious cycle repeated itself. He too was a minister.

In retrospect, I can say I may have been married to the "wrong person" for the "right reasons" considering I was such a young bride. Yet, there are absolutely no regrets for the children birthed from this relationship.

The Dating Scene

Starting over, meeting new people, going on dates--none of it was an easy process for me. I had been married more than half my life. I did not have time to play games, yet I enjoyed doing something different occasionally, with someone different. Dinner here, a movie or two there, hanging out with friends or family of the person I was getting to know was okay. I was still comfortable hanging out with my own family or by myself. I pretty much decided, if I met someone fine, and if I didn't fine. The day I made that statement, the wheels began to turn in the other direction.

A whirlwind courtship

On that fateful Sunday afternoon, August 16, 2009, I went to shop at Wal-Mart, and there was my future getting ready to pass right next to me. To surmise the day, I will include a love note that was written and presented as an anniversary gift to the man I met on our 1st wedding anniversary.

My Dear Vernis,

When I first saw you on Sunday, August, 16, 2009 in Wal-Mart, dressed in your "Sunday Best," you immediately captured my attention. I knew then that there was something extraordinary about you. We greeted one another and went on our merry way. Although, we went into that grocery store that day looking for food/fruit….Fate brought us together! As I was getting into my car, you came out and were parked right next to me. I was truly amazed. Exchanging numbers, you called me a few days later. Afterwards, we had a "whirlwind courtship" and then we were married on December 12, 2009. Wow! And I'm still in love! Happy "1st" Anniversary Baby!

Second Time Around

They say the second time around is better than the first time. Well, let's just say, all relationships require a little work. It also depends on both your motive to be involved in a relationship, and motivation to make the other person happy. It is not always about what *we* want as individuals. It still requires sacrifice. Otherwise, one may as well stay single.

> *"Great spirits have always encountered violent opposition from mediocre minds."*
>
> *Albert Einstein*

There is no such thing as the "perfect" person. I certainly know I am NOT perfect and God only knows he is not either. We have fun together. We love each other, each in our own way, and have different ways of showing it. We are working on fulfilling each other's love language.

There is nothing like having oneness and having peace. It is not easy to accomplish, especially when both people have very strong personalities and are both set in their ways. Nor does it help if one is a little older than the other, and they think that gives them seniority in some special way or another.

We have not arrived yet, but with two mature people, and this being the second time around for both of us, there are still quite a few hurdles to jump over. But, with love being the bearer of all things, there is always hope.

Love always seeks the good in and of the other person. Love endures all things. Love takes time. And with God, all things are possible.

I now know like the old hymnal says, "What a Friend

We Have in Jesus." Truly, I can say, "I've got a friend in Jesus." And so do you.

He (Jesus Christ) was hung up, for my hang ups. And yours.

I realize the dirt I was involved in, at points in my life, could have ended up lying on top of me. I could have died, literally, during some of these moments. I think back on my very first experience of having angels watch over me—so young and innocent at the time. How many other times in my life have they been there, protecting me while I was oblivious to their presence? Perhaps God always knew I needed extra angels, and He loved me enough to place them strategically around me.

Thankfully, God is a God of second chances—and more. May we never take his grace for granted. My pastor once said to me, "I have never seen anyone so resilient, who has gone through as much as you have gone through and bounce back like nothing ever happened." I can only attribute this to grace and mercy following me all the days of my life. Psalm 23:6

May I leave you with these ever important words?

"For God so loved the world that He gave His only begotten Son, that whosoever believeth in Him should not perish, but have everlasting life." John 3:16 (KJV)

"Let us therefore come boldly to the throne of grace, that we may obtain mercy and find grace to help in time of need." Hebrews 4:16 (NKJV)

On that note, I want to share the title of a song that I love—"Falling in Love with Jesus" by Kirk Whalum, The Gospel According to Jazz Chapter II. Loving Jesus is the best thing I've ever done.

May you find your purpose in life and fulfill it.

"Aspire to inspire before you expire." (Anonymous)

We all may not have the same belief system, but there is one book I consider life's roadmap--the Bible.

Basic
Instructions
Before
Leaving
Earth

> *"Our deepest fear is that we are powerful beyond measure. We ask ourselves, who am I to be brilliant, gorgeous, talented, fabulous? Actually, who are you not to be? We were born to make manifest the glory of God that is within us. And as we let our own light shine, we unconsciously give other people permission to do the same."*
>
> *Marianne Williamson*

"Stop Worrying and Invite God into the Details of Your Life

"Go ahead and gain strength through your pain. Grow through your grief, as long as you recognize your ability to overcome adversity is a blessing from God. As you exercise your courage, exercise your faith as well."

~ ***Bruce Bickel and Stan Jantz (*****God is in the Small Stuff: and it all matters*****)***

"Speak up! Don't let this happen to you.

Say something to somebody that can help you. Do NOT keep silent—no matter what that leader says."

~ Arnita Ware

Original Poetry
by
Anita

A Word From Arnita

In this section of the book, you'll find poems I've written at various points in my life. Some pieces carry deep emotions, reflecting the circumstances I was experiencing at the time. I have always enjoyed writing, and I love using poetry as a way to express myself. If you notice a range of emotions between the poems, it's because they come from different moments/seasons and experiences in my life.

As someone who has found comfort in writing poetry, I encourage you to explore ways to express your deepest emotions, **both good and bad.** *Keeping emotions bottled up can be harmful, even for the healthiest minds. Writing can be* **a helpful outlet,** *especially if you have a tendency toward mental health conditions. It can be a trusted* *friend, allowing you to articulate and share thoughts that are hard to express verbally.*

If writing isn't your preferred method of expression, that's perfectly fine. ***But do find an outlet—some healthy and positive way to express what you feel. You'll be glad you did.***

My other outlet is music!

There are two songs that I listened to ***repeatedly*** (on my cassette tape 😁) during this season in my life; once I got out of the hospital in 1988.

Both are by the gospel artist Hezekiah Walker

"I'll Make It" (1987)

The Love Fellowship Crusade Choir

&

"The Lord Will Make a Way Somehow" (1987)

The Love Fellowship Crusade Choir

These two songs kept me **MOTIVATED & ENCOURAGED!**

Peace at the River

Down by the river, one can find peace.
Peace for the soul, where your troubles will cease.

The joyous songs sung by the little birds is
just a simple reminder that your thoughts
and voice can be heard.

Waiting to be heard by God above,
He's also down by the river
Waiting to share his love.

He wraps his love around your soul, mind and heart.
He wants you to cast your burdens upon him
So he can give you a fresh start.

When you take the time, you will find peace at the river
By God himself, the eternal one, the life giver
That is, when you take time to go down by the river.

A Good Morning

The birds, yes, the little birds as small as they may be,
seem to make one of nature's sweetest sounds of melody.

Who can overlook her beauty
when she so sweetly sounds off in the daylight?
One can't help but agree, that her timing of singing,
in the morning, is just right!

God's way of saying, "Good Morning, world,
I've given you a brand new day,
Wake up now and get started on your merry way."

It's a new path, for yesterday is now gone.
You may now make history with the present from this moment on.
And when on the morrow, you arise and shine again, be it God's will,
you will remember each day, He uses the birds to say
"Good Morning" still.

If I Told You

If I told you "I Love You" every day, would you take it for granted?

If I told you "I Love You" rarely, would you long to hear it?

If I told you "I Love You" by my actions, would you even believe me?

Well, I'm telling you, "I Love You," please don't take it for granted.

I'm telling you "I Love You," so you won't long for it, but cherish the memories.

I'm telling you "I Love You," by my actions, so please believe me;

Please believe me when I say
"I Love You"
so you won't have to say, "If she had only told me."

I'm telling you loud and clear "I Love You," so please pay attention.

If You Were Not Here

If you were not here my life would not be the same, instead there would be a hole in my heart where death had left the pain.

If you were not here, who would fill that void in my life? Since each of us has a duty in this world to sew lots of good deeds of kindness, instead of foolishness and strife.

If you were not here, I would want you to know just how much you really meant, and how life is just too short, and that our time should have been cherished even more, and well spent.

But, you are here and it's important in life that I tell you so. I love you here, now and forever, and treasure you more than you'll ever know.

A Strong Black Woman Am I

Brilliant and resilient
Beautiful, bold and lovely to behold
Yes, a strong Black woman am I.

Large or small,
Short or tall
Simply smart, never afraid to make a new start
Yes, a strong Black woman am I.

Challenge me, yes,
Intimidate me, no
Color me happy, care free, and stress free,
But to be down and depressed always
Never, never, not me.
Yes, a strong Black woman am I.

Ever rising to the top and no I won't be stopped...do you know why?
Because.....
Yes, a strong Black woman am I.

An Appointment with Death

I had an appointment with death, but yet in advance, the day of I did not know.

When he approached me, he asked, “Are you ready to go?”

“Ready? Ready?” Said I, “Is there such a thing?”

“Ready or not,” he said, “I must go back from whence I came,

but when I return, it is you with me, I must bring.”

Between Two Hearts

Deeper than the ocean,
Wider than the sea,
is the level of love that exists
between you and me.

No mountain too high,
No valley too low
No distance too far for
Our love to grow.

The sound of your voice is special like no other.
But, nothing takes the place of your presence.
It makes me want our relationship
to go on a little further.

You speak tender words to my heart
That none else could ever proclaim.
They have the most awesome effect,
Especially, when you call my name.

Bound together in heart,
By distance, kept apart.
Yet, when we get together
it's always like a fresh start.

I love you and I need you to be a part
of my life, both now and forever.
No matter what stands between us, in our
hearts, we'll always be together.

Being You

I am good at being me, what about you?
Are you focusing too much on what others do?
You don't have time to waste,
not knowing who you are.
Take time to reflect on yourself,
and know that you are unique by far.

Search deeply and find yourself and yes,
by all means be true.
Take a close look in the mirror and admit
that you could use a little improvement too.

So, work on being you.
Don't try to be who you are not.
You'll never find satisfaction, or peace,
but what you will find, I assure you
is comfort with being you, at least.

The Mind of My Heart

I write you letters by the thousands in my thoughts. There is just so much to say to you; so much to express, mere words would not do justice. How will I ever get over you? Many years later, there/here you are, of course, at some times more than others monopolizing my thoughts. I can't seem to shake it. What is it about you? What did you do that was so different?

There is no reason you've affected me this deeply. You've stolen a big percentage of my heart. I'm sure that even when I'm 75, you'll still have this place. I've really, really, tried and am convinced that the damage is permanent. I can't shake it, no matter how hard I try.

I miss you . . .

Distant Love

Is it true that absence makes the heart grow fonder?
I really don't know and I can't say,
but sometimes I think of you every day.
I think of you more often than you know,
but I can't always let it show.

My true friend you will always be
because you share
a special time of year with me.
It's not the only day you come to mind,
it just happens to be
One of our fondest times.

Although, our friendship is NOT a secret,
for the sake of peace,
Tucked away in my heart is where I should keep it.
A discreet love you will always be,
Deeply seated in my heart of memory.

Just because we may never share a lifetime together,
Doesn't mean we won't be lifetime friends forever.

Love Has a Heart

Love has feelings too.
Love has a heart that just can't be explained.
It experiences the good, the bad and sometimes pain.
Love sometimes gets confused
when someone tries to
take advantage of her and tries to misuse;
she will not be abused.

Love gets angry when one tries to come between
her and her special mate.
Her temper flairs up,
some things she WON'T tolerate.
Come hell or high water, you can try if you want to,
But she'll retaliate.
Some things don't need no explain',
so I suggest you
Let these thoughts permeate.

Don't blame her when you cross the line because
You have already been warned.
She surpassed her limits
because her heart was previously torn.

Why take it lightly

when someone says they love you?
Don't abuse it, don't misuse it.
Don't let it slip away.
Because if you don't treat love right,
she'll leave you one day.

Heartache

There have been lots of nights
when I have stayed awake and cried,
trying to hide my feelings,
no matter how hard I tried.
Why did you have to leave me?
I'll never know,
But now that I have you back,
I will never let you go.

I guess you didn't realize how bad I was hurting,
until, you began to feel it too.
That is most certainly what true love will do to you.

You know we say
we don't miss a good thing till it is gone,
but sometimes, believe it or not,
it just takes the help of a few lyrics of a love song.

Now that you will be forever mine,
the only thing that can
possibly keep us together is time.

A Lunch Date with Myself

Today, I have a very important meeting.
Earlier, I was sitting down eating.
My appetite was very small.
I don't know what to say in this session at all.
I'm at a point of major contemplation in my life,
I'm actually struggling over whether or not
I wish to continue to be his wife.

It's been sometime since I had lunch alone,
At least it gave me a chance to think.
Many thoughts have passed through my mind in 30 minutes,
And some of them have yet to sink.

I'll do it again real soon one day,
Maybe the thoughts of reflection will be much brighter, I pray.

The Legacy

Every day, every day, every day . . . is a journey. What shall
we do with the time that we have?
How much do we really value life?
Does it really make a difference?
Why of course it does.
Each of us has an opportunity
to make a difference in the life of another person, whether
good or bad.
If one chooses to donate his goods to the poor,
he has made a difference in the life of another.
If one chooses to rape, steal, or murder,
it makes a difference.

The question is,
what type of legacy will you or I leave
when all is said and done?
I once read a statement that said,
you should live a life so much
so that even the funeral director will be saddened that
you're gone.
That's a pretty powerful life.
Let's live each day to the fullest;
love to the highest degree.

The Learning Process

From the day we are born, until the day we die, there is so much in life to learn, or at least try.

Will we ever get an understanding of why we've gone through the way we have? God only knows.
I want to believe that I've learned from my past experiences, and that they've helped me to grow.
Sometimes, it hurts too bad to feel like you were actually supposed to get something out of it.

I've gone through a lot in only 37 years.
I have a few nuggets I could share with society. Some of the experiences I've had, not even people twice my age have ever had, nor will they ever have. Does that make me a better person or worse? No, not necessarily. Nonetheless, I must make a conscious decision to move forward.

Sometimes, I am at a very difficult place in my life in making decision that could affect my entire future. Are some things worth the risk? Is true love even worth the risk? That's personal. Go figure! I guess whatever is meant to be will happen? Or do we interfere and make it happen? Some things will simply be between two hearts.

Should I Hate?

Hate you? Hate you?
Because you betrayed me?
No, I wish you no ill.
But I visualize drama, if you
Dare try again still.

I do not want to see you
Hear you, touch you,
Let alone smell you near
For my level of anger
Will cause you to
Taste of fear.

Fear that you are
In danger of your
Life, if you ever consider
Causing anymore
Dissention, in my
Home or strife.

If you want to
Hate me, go ahead
For with you, I have
Nothing else to lose
But from this time
Forward, I will
Be much more selective
With the friends I choose.

Just Because You Are My Mother

It means so much having you in my life,
To have known, and know you as my mother.
Your friendship means more to me than any other.

You have instilled such Godly principals and standards to live by,
Just simply reflecting, brings tears to my eyes.

Your example of a Godly woman stood out to me,
It persuaded me to pattern after you. In doing so, I ended up doing what God has called me to do.

Living, loving, serving, with my whole heart,
all because my mother gave me an opportunity to start.
A seed was planted long ago, when you took me with you to share a prayer, to help and serve others.
Now, I'm still working in the kingdom
Helping other sisters and brothers.

Your friendship and loyalty has proven itself more and more.
As the need arises, you are there for me like an opportunity,
So, I open the door.
Thanks for being there when I've needed you most,

You seem to take such pleasure in doing wonderful
things for others, similar to a host.

Your deeds are so unique and so kind,
I wouldn't have anyone else for my mother,
if you don't mind.

You are my mother!
Just because you are my mother,
May I give you your flowers while you live,
while you can see and smell them
and while I can now give.

Thanks for being a "precious" mother!

I Love You Much!

The Struggle Inside of You

I've passed this way many times with you before,
And now I just cannot seem to take it anymore.
It really hurts me to have to deal with you this way,
but there is only so much I can say.

I've expressed my disappointment to you,
in how you've let yourself go.
You need to get some serious help,
it is passed time for you to grow.
If you don't get control of yourself,
you will lose everyone and
Everything that is precious to you,
Including me, that is, if indeed it is true.

You're at an age that you should be settling down,
But you're in such bad shape, people are starting to
NOT want you around.
It's not "you" they don't want,
but your monster inside,
As you let him reside.
Remember, Satan seeks whom he "MAY" devour,
Which means, he needs your permission,
But, if I were you, I wouldn't allow him to keep me
Suppressed, depressed, oppressed, in that condition.

You have no idea what it is like being on the outside of you, looking in;
All these years, I've only tried to be a true friend.
On the other hand, I don't know what it is like being on the inside of you, looking out.
Maybe, it really is scary,
but you must trust the Lord
To change your life, no doubt.

My relationship with you is causing me unnecessary stress;
I can't deny that I really care.
But the burden of it is so much more than I can bear.
I have tried so hard
not to completely rid myself of you,
But now, I'm not quite sure of what I will do.

You say you care about your friends and loved ones dear,
Yet, you keep doing the same ole thing, year after year.
As of today, I am holding you accountable and responsible
For getting yourself together,
Least you lose your once-in-a-lifetime friend, forever.

Only a true friend will tell you what is right or what is good for you,
The question is, can you handle the truth?
And if so, what are you going to do???

I Knew I Loved You When . . .

I knew I loved you when . . . with your first kiss, you took my breath away, and I wanted you to stay.

I knew I loved you when . . . again, you kissed me, and my entire body wilted and became a limp noodle.

I knew I loved you when . . . you showed up unexpectedly, out of the blue, with a gift.

I knew I loved you when . . . each time, you patiently listened; to hear me express my joys and sorrows.

I knew I loved you when . . . you repeatedly supported me, while I furthered my education. You encouraged my personal growth and passions.

I knew I loved you when . . . we stood in the pouring rain; unlocking the gate, then you made love to me, and I called your name.

I knew I loved you when . . . we danced together in true harmony, in sync, with one rhythm. Our hearts and souls became a symphony.

I knew I loved you when . . . we spent our first night together, and it was clear my soul loved your soul. I could feel the fire burning within and without.

I Knew I Loved You!

I . . .
I knew . . .
I knew I . . .
I knew I loved . . .
I knew I loved you!
When?

I knew I loved you when . . . I realized I appreciate every little thing you do, and I'm fortunate to have you.

I knew I loved you when . . . I realized your intelligence is so attractive, and I love the way your mind works, and that I would choose you over and over again.

I *Knew* I Loved You!

Dearest Jesus

Dearest Jesus,

I know that I have not been perfect, in all of my holy days. At some point I was distracted, and I ceased to follow your ways. Knowing right from wrong, I still went astray, but I'm so glad you were there to help me find my way. The conviction of your spirit is always right and true, and helps to guide us along the way, when we don't know what else to do.

Condemnation has played it's part in trying to hold me back, but I will go on in Christ, and that is just a fact. I'm so glad you chose me to be a worthy child, even though Satan yet tries to tempt me, all the while. I realize that his intents are true. He wants me to be destroyed and burn in Hell with him too.

I will not cease to praise you, regardless of what trial comes my way. I shall forever seek to praise you each and every day. As I await your miraculous and glorious return, and I know you're soon to come, my very soul longs to see you, but in the meantime, I'll work, until the day is done.

Original
Short Stories
by
Anita

The Bible is right when it says in Corinthians 4:8-9, "We are troubled on every side, yet not distressed; we are perplexed, but not in despair, persecuted, but not forsaken; cast down, but not destroyed…" And in II Corinthians 12:10, "…for Christ's sake…for when I am weak, then am I strong."

Louise and Sherry are having one of their occasional girls' day out. Sherry catches Louise daydreaming after they take a stroll to the lake. Louise is reflecting over her painful divorce, and tells Sherry about disappointments she experiences at times, and all of the aftermath that comes with the territory of a divorce.

Sherry agrees with Louise when she says that on the other hand she refuses to have a pity party!

"Yeah! High Five Baby!"

The girls carry on about how beautiful life really is, and it is way too short to horde bitterness in the heart.

Both of these ladies are strong African-American women who are very business minded and don't mind working to make things happen. You say work, and they are there. They are always encouraging one another to strive for more and the best of any and everything.

Sherry lists all the things that Louise has already accomplished and is in the process of accomplishing by reminding her how far she has come in such a short span of time—three years. She insists that Louise keep moving forward to pursue all of her dreams, even though she thought they would be accomplished during her marriage.

Louise makes a suggestion to Sherry that she can't refuse—a road trip. To New Orleans they will go. Louise is going to visit all of her aunts who are all sassy, single, and in their 70's. Yes, her aunts had been married before, but it didn't work out. Louise figures she can go sit at the feet of the "old school" ladies and have a couple of "fireside chats" and learn a little something, something! Sherry is ecstatic. When is the trip, she wants to know.

The trip is a huge success. Louise learns things about her aunts that she never knew, all starting from the usual girls day out. Louise and Sherry can't wait to see what the next one will bring. Maybe it will be a bus tour with a whole group of ladies going to Vegas or somewhere!

Daddy

There he stood, the one and only Robert Earl Portis, affectionately known as Bob, staring out of the kitchen window. It appeared his dove-like eyes were fixed on the garden, or was he simply gazing into space? Next to dozing on the couch while he watched wrestling, boxing, westerns, or some show of excitement or another, the kitchen was his favorite hangout. Daddy loved to eat.

He was a tall gentleman with big, broad shoulders, whose teeth sparkled like ivory and gold when his big grin stretched a mile wide across his face. He was wearing an old pair of faded blue jeans with a hole or two in them that he wore when he went fishing, which was one of his favorite sports. His other passion was hunting. His hair was now black with more metallic gray throughout his entire head, yet the texture was as soft as cotton.

Daddy had a gentle voice. He was soft spoken, yet ever so firm. Rarely, did he have to raise his voice, because his body language would always confirm his seriousness. Every now and then, when Mama wouldn't quit fussing about one little thing or another, he would speak up and say, "All right, now. Hush woman."

If for some reason she had trouble understanding him, as if she didn't hear him the first time, he would simply repeat himself and say, "I said, hush now."

His patience was immeasurable. I always admired his

tolerance. Naturally, I asked him why he was looking out the window.

He turned to me and said, "I'm trying to decide if I'm going to fry this fish this evening. If so, I need some help with scaling, gutting, and cleaning them up."

I volunteered my services, because I knew I was ready to eat.

Usually, Daddy would have already yelled out, "Nita, come here, I've got a job for you!" Boy did we dread those words. No telling what Daddy had up his sleeve. It was always a family affair when he had work for you to do. He asked Mama to cook some biscuits to go with the fish.

We lived in the Deep South, in New Orleans, Louisiana. Daddy was from Cuba, Alabama, which is not exactly on the map, but is next to Meridian, Mississippi. We always had several cans of good ole country cane syrup in the house, to go with the biscuits. It was one of our favorites. We conversed, finished cleaning and cooking the fish, and had a wonderful dinner, as usual. Delicious!

I now look back with fond memories of my dad.

Every Day was Secretary's Day

There was a time when I thought a revolving door only applied to hotels and fancy restaurants. I soon learned it also applies to school systems, too. I applied for a job as elementary school secretary and got it. I was the only applicant.

The previous school secretary and clerk quit without warning. I soon found out why. The principal and assistant principal were fairly new to the school, and the teachers were running the show. They were out of control, running the building, and accustomed to being in charge. They must have thought they were at Burger King where you can "Have It Your Way."

All summer long, shipments of classroom supplies came in. There were boxes everywhere, from the floor to the ceiling. There was no order, no structure anywhere to be found.

"This teacher workroom is a mess," I fussed under my breath like a mother hen. "I can't believe this is an elementary school. If someone had told me it looked this bad I wouldn't have believed it."

School was about to start and there were still basic supplies to be ordered—pencils, pens, Xerox paper, scissors, tape. You name it, whatever a teacher needs to run a classroom. Students were still registering for school, and all of their information had to be input into the computer. The building was still under renovation. Work orders needed completion, and keys needed distributing to every classroom and outside door. I had my work cut out for me.

I'll never forget the day that Darlene, my principal, introduced me as the new school secretary at our first school beginning of the year, faculty meeting.

"Arnita's reputation precedes her," she said. "She is a very organized person, an efficient professional, and knows how to run a school. She has influence with all the right people and can work miracles."

Darlene went on and on, and I wanted to crawl up under a chair. It was bad enough that I could feel all eyes on me. This campus had its own personality. Just like a home has a certain atmosphere, so does a school. Boy, were there some serious attitudes in the room!

Before school started, I had a plan to get rid of all boxes. Then I met Chelsey, the ring leader of the teacher's group.

"We are going to go through the boxes and take what belongs to our grade level or department," she said.

"No ma'am. Thanks for offering your assistance, but I have a plan," I responded politely. "I assure you that each one of you will have your boxes in your classroom when you return on next week. Thank you for the opportunity to let me take of this."

The other teachers surrounding Chelsey looked at me in amazement. They were all afraid to speak up for themselves and had never witnessed anyone standing up to Chelsey. My next challenge was getting information in the computer.

"Darlene," I said. "I am going to need some help in getting these students registered in the computer."

Daisy, our assistant principal, who was painting a red

wall in her new office, yelled out from her room, "Maybe we can call someone from Central Office to come and help us since we still have to hire two clerks before school starts."

"That's a bright idea," I replied.

So I made a few phone calls and explained our dilemma. We did get a couple of people to come to our campus to help us register students while I worked along with them. This helped me complete a few other tasks, too.

I was not omnipresent. There were times when I needed to be at my desk, in the teacher workroom, and in the restroom taking a potty break at the same time. So much had to be done. Enroll and withdraw students, talk to parents, vendors, administrators; count money, answer the phones, make phone calls, help the substitutes, type memos, send notes home with students; order supplies, organize workroom, input work orders, maintain all budgets, and the list goes on.

Someone always needed something. If it wasn't the principal, it was the we-will-not-follow-instructions teachers. One morning, Mr. Martin, the head custodian, came to me at the front desk in the office.

"I need more supplies, please," he said. "I am low on bathroom tissue."

"Bathroom tissue is not something to run out of," I replied. "You are now at the top of my list."

Ten cases of bathroom tissue were delivered that afternoon.

Six weeks after school started, Mrs. McDonald, the art teacher, said to me, "Where have you been all of these years? We now have a laminator, binding machine, and scan Tron machine. We've never had so many supplies."

Mrs. Appleton, the nurse, chimed in, "I've received a washer, dryer, a patient bed, and built-in storage to keep spare clothes."

Mr. Martin rounded the corner just in time to add, "I received a new flatbed to haul several bags of trash at a time. Arnita also ordered rugs to go beneath the drinking fountains."

"What's the big deal?" I said. "That's a safety issue."

When it was all said and done, the doors didn't revolve as often. The rate of student and staff transfers were down. Everyone was on board. I fell in love with the campus, and everyone loved me and respected my position as school secretary.

Love Don't Pay the Bills

Tina Turner said it best when she sang "What's Love Got to Do with It?"

Every one of us has learned to some degree that one of the biggest causes of relationship break-ups is financial difficulties. One would think it's understood that everyone knows the necessity of paying bills, and that it takes lots of funds to run a household and have a secure financial future.

What man wants a woman that wants to spend all of the money to buy a new pair of shoes each week or get new hairstyles or her nails done when the lights are turned off?

What woman wants to be told how much she is loved by her man, but he just won't work. If you don't work, you won't eat, or so it goes according to Scripture.

In an average household, both parties should provide an ample salary. It wouldn't hurt to make sure that you and your spouse share the same financial values before deciding to tie the knot. There really needs to be an agreement on the importance of credit worthiness, as well as job stability.

Sometimes the routine of paying bills or planning for the future can feel overwhelming, but it's unwise not to plan for retirement, education for the children, and death expenses. Who wants to inherit even more debt due to poor planning or no planning at all?

Take for example the story of one couple that lost the head of the household due to an untimely death. Forty-six year-old Daniel was at the hospital visiting his father who had just recently had surgery. While talking to his father, he had a massive heart attack and died on the spot. There was insurance money for burial, but that's all. There wasn't enough money to take care of paying off the house and all other expenditures.

Another account to consider is the experience of a young couple. Leroy and his wife, Danielle, had only been married five years, and Leroy was already very unhappy. He had a wife, but not a life.

Frustrated, he said to Danielle, "You promised to take care of this bill again! Can I not trust you to use the money wisely? We have bills to pay."

Nothing Leroy did seemed to work. He and his wife tried to keep steady jobs, but things did not seem to work out for one reason or another.

"I don't want to talk about this right now," Danielle said. "That's all you talk about is money! I want to party and have some fun. You need to learn to relax."

"No, the problem is you're too relaxed," Leroy responded. "You don't seem to give a flying flip about anything that matters."

"Well, if you love me, you would let me go shopping," Danielle murmured.

Leroy had given up all of his dreams to marry this chick. She claimed that she had dreams too, but it seemed that her immediate dream was to convince someone to marry her and take care of her and her child from a previous relationship, just to get from under her mother's thumb. Once they were married, she confirmed her immaturity by neglecting to pay the bills with the money Leroy entrusted to her to handle, since he was the primary bread winner.

Danielle worked also, but for a minimal salary. They moved over and over, from pillar to post, because they couldn't seem to make ends meet enough to keep a roof over their heads—a lifestyle Leroy was definitely not accustomed to. Stability was all he knew, although this was the norm for Danielle and her family. She ended up right back where she came from, her mother's home. The couple decided to split up and make some decisions about which direction they needed to take with their lives as individuals, before they could determine if they would be successful as a couple.

Financial stability is crucial in today's economic crunch, whether a person is married or single.

Not only is it beneficial, but it's necessary to live a prudent lifestyle in order to survive. If people learn to live within their means, all will be well—not only for individuals, but for families, too. No sense in trying to keep up with the Jones'. There is a quote that says "A lot of people are in debt because they spend what their friends think they make." This sums it up in a nutshell. Life is simple. It isn't as difficult as we make it seem. It's just a matter of handling your business. Perhaps we should take the Nike approach and "Just Do It."

The cost of living has skyrocketed. To survive in these times, a person has to first love themselves enough to be willing to make a decent living—before taking on the responsibility and added pressure of another person. Discipline and responsibility are the keys to living an adult life. Love alone is not enough to keep the chill out of the house in the middle of the winter if there is no money to pay the electric bill.

Children can't begin to relate to this. They simply know they are uncomfortable and want to feel warm, cozy, safe, and secure at home. Parents are obligated to take care of their children and provide for their comfort and well-being. And that's where the love comes in.

Love Interrupted by Tragedy

In thinking of the power of influence and love, it is very difficult to do without remembering Mary Coleman and Gertie Perkins.

Mother Mary Coleman, as she was called by the members of the church, had spark and pizazz. Although, her husband had long passed, it never slowed her down a bit. She was always at choir rehearsal on time and faithful to her position as choir president. She always had a smile on her face and peppermints in her purse to share with others. She sang "tenor" in the choir and was known for being one of the song leaders. But, she could also sing soprano. She was well known in the city of New Orleans at the jazz fest under the gospel tent for singing a song entitled "Traveling Shoes."

She always stretched out her long arms for a big hug of affection. She had a sense of humor too, and always had some sort of wise crack to say here or there. Well, these things came to a screeching halt one Wednesday night when we were expecting her at church. The head deacon that stopped by her home as usual to pick her up, came to church that night without her and with horrific news. The pastor was up speaking as the deacon walked up to the pulpit and whispered in the Pastor's ear. With one unified sound, the congregation moaned, when the announcement came. Mother Coleman had been found dead. I felt especially shocked, as she sat right next to me during choir rehearsals and church services.

The New Orleans local newspaper The Times Picayune reported that her attacker beat her in the head with a heavy frying pan and apparently stole her purse. The 25-year-old woman who was living with her and cooked for her was not home at the time of the incident.

Her body was found around 8p.m. on her bedroom floor by a church deacon who came to give hear a ride to a revival service. One of the ladies she used to sing with in a gospel quartet said she was a very funny lady and had a beautiful personality. I can attest to that.

When Mary Coleman stopped singing with the Jackson Gospel singers after 20 years, she joined and performed with the gospel choir of the First Church of God in Christ in New Orleans. She was one of the most active church members, even at the age of 76. Even her pastor stated that she was at the church nearly every time the doors were opened.

Ironically, both my mother and I had different dreams related to this death. My mother dreamed of someone being murdered. In the dream, she saw a person being hit in the head with an object, hands above her head trying to protect herself. This is the position Mary Coleman was found in.

I dreamed of a very large funeral where there was standing room only. Not many days after we had these dreams (more like nightmares), this tragedy come to pass.

As if this was not enough of an experience, I wonder to this day why people who lived such beautiful lives had to go out in this manner.

Now to honor the memory of Gertie Perkins, another elderly woman who did not always seem so elderly because she was so full of life. But she was 64 years old. Gertie was a school bus driver, restaurant owner, manager of the family business GM Perkins Trucking Company, wife, loving mother and cherished by many in her church and community. She sat one pew across from me each Sunday at church. She always looked over and smiled, but you could never pass by her without getting a good "smooch." She was going to kiss you, ready or not. That was her way of saying, "I love you." She was an example of love and kindness. She was a model for the younger women. She always had a word of encouragement.

Did she deserve to be loved back? I would certainly say, yes. However, the Fort Worth Star Telegram reported the following incident in Dec. 2000:

"A Fort Worth Family's Agony Wait Ends in Sorrow…..Body of Missing Woman is Found.

'A 64-year-old woman reported missing by her family Monday was found dead Tuesday night in the trunk of her car in a parking garage,' police said. 'A relative led investigators to the car in the garage of the former St. Joseph Hospital, 1400 S. Main St, around 9 p.m.,' Lt. Mark Krey said."

She was reported missing by her husband, Willie, when she failed to pick up their great-grandson from school. There were injuries that were consistent with foul play. The relative who had been jailed earlier that Tuesday for failing to register as a sex offender was being questioned by police, when he led them to the car. Her husband kept picturing her tied up in the car, maybe in the trunk. He insisted they needed to find her. The inside of her meticulous home in Southeast Fort Worth was found in disarray on that Monday afternoon. A piece of carpet was cut away in the bedroom. The bed linens and pillows had been stripped off and taken. Gertie Perkins purse, a check and her 1998 champagne color Cadillac were missing.

Another article heading read as follows: "Stepson is arrested in the slaying of a woman, 64. 'He strangled her, stashed the body in the trunk of her car and left it in a hospital garage,' police say"

Although both their lives ended horribly, these women left a legacy of love.

On the Road Again

It was a warm, clear, sunny Friday morning in August when the girls, Sherry and Louise, decided it was time for "the road trip." Finally, they were going to head to see Louise's aunts and Mother. The distance from the Dallas metroplex to New Orleans was approximately 550 miles.

"Oh, I am so ready. Let's do this!" Louise blurted out.

"I'm with ya girl, let's roll," Sherry agreed.

Previously, Louise and Sherry had talked about going to New Orleans to meet Louise's aunts so they could sit and be taught a few things by the "old school" ladies. Louise's aunts were very strong and independent, and she knew she and Sherry would fit right in, likely benefitting from their wisdom. They were two young women just daring to try something new.

"Girl, we'd better get some pep in our step and get to the grocery store to stock up on some road trip goodies, then get the car packed so we can get out of here," Louise pointed out.

"Now, that's what I'm talking about." Sherry laughed. "That's my kind of traveling buddy. Hey Louise, have you ever heard this quote before? 'There ain't no surer way to find out whether or not you like people or hate them than to travel with them?'"

"No. But it sure makes sense. Who said that?"

"Mark Twain. Happy Birthday, Louise."

"Why, thanks Sherry." Louise grinned.

"You know what? I did not realize when you said we'd be leaving on Friday, August 5th, that it would fall on your birthday."

"Well, you know me." Louise shrugged. "I usually have a plan. I just thought it would make the weekend more meaningful to spend it with a good friend and my family."

They started driving. As they conversed, while listening to music, snacked, napped, and took a couple of restroom breaks, several hours passed.

"Hey Sherry, do you ever think about how fast the years are flying by, and that we are getting older? I mean, we were both in our 20's when we met." Louise looked over at Sherry. "Do you ever think about dying? Not as if you are afraid, but just that someday we will?"

"Well… To answer your tons of questions, sometimes I do." Sherry frowned and stared out at the highway ahead. "I mostly think of my children and at what age I might be when it happens, as well as how. I wonder if I will go peacefully in my sleep or not. I really don't dwell on it. I know when it happens, I'm ready to meet my Maker. Why, do you ask?" Sherry turned to look at Louise.

"Oh, ummmh, it's just that death is actually a part of life, and sometimes I just wonder if anyone else ever really thinks about it too. " Louise steered the car carefully around a big truck. "For instance, I've noticed that my mom's hair has gotten quite a bit grayer. It makes me realize how precious life is and how important it is to value our family and take advantage of the time we have with them. Life is way too short not to! That's really why I wanted to make this trip. Since, my mom is the youngest of her siblings, and some of them are still living, I want to enjoy each of them while I can."

"Well, I tell ya what, I've worked up an appetite listening so intently to you over there in the passenger seat, Louise. Would you please fix another sandwich for me?"

"Sure, I'd be glad to, 'cause I'm hungry myself." Louise reached for the cooler. "And I'll be ready to drive at any point now since we're getting close, and this is where I always enjoy the driving, bringing the ole' girl in. She's a reliable car. Right around Baton Rouge is my spot!" Louise handed Sherry her sandwich.

"No prob, Bob. Have at it! In fact this really would be a good stopping point. I'll pull off at Glorius Road—exit 432B. We can put some "tiger in the tank" and head on in, since we just have a couple of hours left." Sherry steered toward the off ramp.

"My thoughts exactly," said Louise.

Two hours later, they pulled into the old neighborhood.

"Finally! We've succeeded. Thankfully, we've had a safe journey." Louise parked and turned off the car. "Let's go inside to see Mother."

Although, Louise still had a key to her mama's house, she rang the doorbell several times for the fun of it.

"What do you want, Lil' Girl?" Louise's mom, Arbrie, flung the door open so wide, hitting the door stopper as it made a sound of its own. Bong, yong, yong, yong. "Come on in here and give me some sugah!"

She hugged her daughter and her friend and ushered the two women into the kitchen." How ya doing, Baby? I'm so happy to see y'all. Have a seat. Are you hungry?"

The last one is always a question on the lips of a New

Orleanian that has company. They would probably ask an enemy whether or not he was hungry. Since the girls were a bit worn from the trip, Louise's mom suggested they rest a spell, and perhaps by the time they got up, they could have dinner.

Later on, Louise's aunts were coming over to see her. At last, the time had come for the big gathering! Sherry was going to meet the infamous aunts of Louise!

Waking up from their long nap, Sherry stretched. "Oooh wee! Boy, does that seafood smell good," she said.

"Yes indeed!" replied Louise. They followed the scrumptious scent to the kitchen.

There were trays and trays of boiled crabs, crawfish, shrimp, potatoes, corn on the cob, and even fried catfish.

"Alright, alright! It's time to eat," Arbrie shouted across the room. "Come and get your bellies full."

"My goodness, this is only my first day here." Sherry filled her plate. 'If I keep this up, I'm going to be in big trouble. This food is awesome!"

They laughed and joked and told all kinds of funny and serious stories about when they were growing up and when they were married.

"You all are so funny. Now, I see where Louise gets her sassiness from," said Sherry, her hands full of crab.

"Yeah, well, we've gotta enjoy each other while we can," stated Aunt Glorie. "We're getting older and y'all will have to carry on the next generations."

She was trying to impress upon the girls how important it is to spend quality time with your family and love everybody. She had been diagnosed with cancer, but had not yet revealed it to her family.

"Hope you girls are not too busy to go to church and serve the Lord. We surely have to meet our Maker, and we need to be prepared. Let's be sure to pray together as a family before we all depart tonight," Aunt Glorie added.

While they continued eating, Aunt Lavada kept asking Louise every few minutes, how her husband was doing. But, Louise was so busy listening to Aunt Glorie that she didn't really pay attention to how many times she asked the question. As usual, Aunt Sylvie was going back to get more of whatever was being served, and clowning around while she was at it. Louise's mom just enjoyed the company.

Although the weekend went fast, and in spite of the dreadful news that Louise received about her aunt's cancer, the girls still had a great time. Louise learned that not only did her Aunt Glorie have cancer, her Aunt Lavada now had Alzheimer's disease, and Aunt Sylvie, already diabetic, was going to have a toe amputated soon. Arbrie, Louise's mom had just recently started having really sharp pains shoot through her legs and back on a regular basis. It was a sure sign that the trip was meant to be. It helped both Louise and Sherry recognize and deeply appreciate the value of family and friends. The girls promised to do whatever they could to help them through their transitions and promised they would start taking better care of themselves, especially while they were still somewhat young. The "old school ladies" forced Louise and Sherry to promise with their pinkies.

Louise and Sherry headed back to Texas with very mixed emotions. They surmised that the purpose of their trip was to learn a few things from the "old school" ladies, and they did. They were told how important it is to take care of their bodies and be more health conscience while they are young and have the ability to help prevent illness. They also realized it is not just quantity of time with family, but quality time that matters most. They made a commitment to one another that they would start a foundation for young women to become more in touch with themselves—spirit, soul, and body—and to become educated and influential in life.

Louise promised Sherry she would teach the younger ones to live a life of such a great legacy, that even the funeral director would be sad when they passed away.

The trip left an indelible impression that will last for years to come.

The No-Nonsense Neighbor

It was a superb, sunny afternoon when suddenly the snow white clouds began to blacken as if they were charcoaled on a grill, and the sky turned gloomy. Tony was headed inside after picking up some trash when he saw his neighbor, Ms. Lavonne, walking down the street with several bags of groceries. As usual, Tony ran over to offer his assistance.

"Hey, Miz Lavonne," he said, taking the bags from her with a smile. "Let me help you get these inside before it starts raining."

"Oh, thank you, Tony." Ms. Lavone smiled back at him gratefully. "I don't know what Lionel and I would do without you."

"It's nothing, Miz Lavonne," Tony said modestly. "Lionel is my bud."

Tony was sixteen, popular, and well-respected in the neighborhood. His strong athletic build spoke for itself. He was as muscular as the Incredible Hulk, except he wasn't green, and had a manner about him that said, "Don't mess with me, and if you do, I've got something for ya." If Tony was on your side, you'd better believe he was on your side! He stopped at nothing for those he cared about most.

Ms. Lavonne enlisted Tony's help when it was time to send her son, Lionel, who had a speech impediment, to

Gensen's, the neighborhood corner store. Although he was twenty-four years old, he was a special needs individual. Since his older brother had grown up and left home, and his sister Debbie had drowned a few years earlier, Lionel had become very afraid of going by himself. Tony understood that Lionel needed to feel secure again, and as far as Tony was concerned, when it came to Lionel, "don't even think about it!"

A few of the neighborhood kids thought it was amusing to tease Lionel when he ventured to Gensen's alone. When Ms. Lavonne brought this to Tony's attention, he took it upon himself to walk with Lionel to build up his confidence. The kids knew they could only get away with teasing Lionel when Tony wasn't around.

One day Tony was returning home, he rounded the corner and saw the pack of kids who loved to tease Lionel running away from Ms. Lavonne's home. Lionel was sitting on the steps, staring into oblivion and looking very sad.

Tony went up to him and said "Don't worry, I'll take care of them, Lionel."

Later, he found the pack of kids who had been picking on Lionel, marched right up to them and said, "If I ever see you annoying Lionel again, you are going to seriously be in a world of trouble. You will get five of these where you sneeze!" Five of these indicated his fist, and where you sneeze meant he would sock them right on the nose. "And that is not a threat, it's a promise."

Tony didn't believe in taking advantage of another person's weakness. Lionel learned from the best and was eventually able to go to the store alone.

Besides Lionel, Ms. Lavonne also had two nieces that

visited frequently in the summer. One of them, Arnetria, was the apple of Tony's eye. She was special to him, and beautiful to behold. Her sexy, slim, silhouette was always a colorful and vivid portrait in his mind.

Tony and Arnetria would sit on the porch and talk and laugh, or sometimes they would just hang out in the hallway looking out the window together there in the apartment building. Ms. Lavonne lived on the second floor, Apt. C on St. Thomas St. in New Orleans. Tony lived across the driveway on the third floor—Apt. F on Adele St.

When it was time to say goodnight, Tony would give Arnetria a gentle kiss on the cheek. She'd stay in the window and watch him walk across the driveway. Sometimes, if they had more to say, he'd call her, and they'd stay on the phone, looking out the window at each other across the alley while they talked. Tony had a romantic side only Arnetria knew about.

He really loved this girl, but instead of expressing his feelings, he pondered them in his heart for a long time. He said to himself, while walking home across the alley one night, "I really love this girl, but it's not time to tell her yet. One day, I'm going to ask her to marry me."

One evening, Tony and Arnetria took a stroll to the park. They held hands while they walked and talked and laughed about everything under the sun. He admitted to her how important her cousin Lionel and her aunt Ms. Lavonne were to him. They giggled their way under a large shade tree. Their smiles became serious.

"The stars sparkle in your sweet sensitive eyes, Arnetria," Tony softly said to her.

She had that bashful little girl look in her eyes. He could

no longer resist, and smack dab in the middle of the park, he gently kissed her lips. Without doubt, it was clearly understood from that moment on, Arnetria and Tony, the no-nonsense neighbor, would always be together. They were truly in love.

About the Author

Arnita's life has been a tapestry of challenges and triumphs, where she's learned firsthand that "life happens" beyond our control. Through the darkness and difficult seasons, she credits God for carrying her through, much like the Footprints in the Sand. She has learned to ***accept what God allows***. Her journey is a testament to resilience and faith, inspiring others along the way.

Her unique narrative includes a profound discovery of a mental health condition, shaped by divine protection since her youth. Though public humiliations have tested her trust in people, ***her faith in God has only grown stronger.***

Arnita wears many hats: She is the founder of Just Write since 2007 - ***www.justwrite4insight.com***
She is an Author, Educator, Mental Health and Wellness Life Coach/Mental Health Advocate. In addition, she is a Speaker and a member of the International Association of Professional Writers & Editors, Professional Organization of Women of Excellence Recognized, The Society for Collegiate Leadership and Achievement & Lifetime member of Strathmore's Who's Who Worldwide. She holds a Bachelor of Applied Arts & Sciences degree from Lamar University in Beaumont, Texas.

Above all, reflecting on her deep-rooted values as ***a member of the "Body of Christ,"*** her commitment to writing extends *beyond writing just to write.*

She has a passion for writing and is also a columnist for the Fort Worth Black News where she is committed to delivering "the good news." www.dfwblacknews.com The ***Amen*** Corner (Faith & Inspiration)

Beyond her professional accomplishments, Arnita is family-oriented and spirit-led, cherishing her roles as a mother, daughter, sister, and friend. Known affectionately as Mimi to her grandchildren, she finds joy in music, traveling, painting, cooking, reading, and writing.

She is passionate about helping others reach their fullest potential through intentional self-care. She believes that **personal wellness** *is the foundation for* **effectively supporting and pouring into others.**

She is a strong advocate for mental health and wellness, offering her time and service to the community. She understands that too many people are living on the edge, unaware of how close they are to crisis . . . much closer to breaking than they realize . . . silently struggling.

Even if/when they do recognize it . . . fear, shame, stigma and embarrassment keep them from reaching out for the help they deserve.

It's okay to NOT be okay.

Her goal is to help **de-stigmatize** *mental health,*

and assure others…that they are **NOT ALONE.**

For more information, you can reach Arnita at:

JustWrite4Insight@Gmail.com

www.justwrite4insight.com

Thank you so much for reading my book! If you have purchased from an online platform, please… kindly leave a review.

More importantly, if you know of others who would truly benefit from reading this book, please share its title with them.

I appreciate your support.

www.ingramcontent.com/pod-product-compliance
Lightning Source LLC
La Vergne TN
LVHW010926110826
845149LV00013B/2495

9798994438411